“Breaking The Shackles”

Empowering your Body, Mind and Spirit to Unchain to the Rythym

Denis Ahern

"You alone have a vision of how your life should be or where you want it to go, no one else can see it or even understand it like you do. Trust it and do not leave other people's visions or opinions of where you should be or what you should be doing, impair your vision"

Contents

INTRODUCTION

I write in a different manner to most other people. I do not dedicate a certain time each day or have a dedicated place that I go to do it. For me when I write, it is all a series of messages that I receive that get the point across that I or others need to hear.

These messages come to me when I could be out for a run, driving down the road, watching tv, meditating or meeting clients. It is not that I am purposely putting out the intention to receive them, they come when they need to be heard.

The messages that form this book are normally given to me at times when I need it the most or when people close to me need it.

They are messages from a world that I never quite understand but I have complete trust in, from a team that I will be forever a student learning from the masters, from guides who always direct me onto the right path and from an energy that always protects me no matter what.

It was through my own journey of taking a more holistic approach in understanding my own physical, mental and emotional health that led me to rediscover myself.

It helped me to rediscover the part of me that I had hidden away for so long, a part of me that I had completely forgotten existed, the part of me that I had to hide in order to fit into a world that I could never fit into. The part of me that I am only fully beginning to embrace.

Breaking the Shackles will give you the ability to break free from all that you think that you are, giving you the freedom to take back your own power, owning who you are and embracing what the future holds for you, knowing without a shred of doubt that everything will be ok.

It is the breaking free of all judgements, thought forms and misconceptions that you may have in order to create a life for you that is full of wonder and possibilities, realising that you are fully protected at all times.

Breaking the Shackles will give you the key to unlock all the chains that you have been tied to - physically, mentally, emotional and spiritually, helping you to unchain to the rhythm of the world that you have become so accustomed to, to live your best life, the life that you truly deserve.

PREFACE

THE HUMAN ENERGY FIELD / THE AURA

Every single human being is a ball of energy, not just the physical kind. Apart from having our own energy, we are giving out and receiving different energies all the time.

Whilst some energies are helpful, others aren't. In simple terms one person or place might make you feel happy whilst another might drain you physically, mentally and emotionally.

If you look at energy the way you look at fingerprints, everything you touch you leave your print on, so energy works in the same way, every person that you meet, every thought that you have and everyplace that you go, are all taking parts of your energy, whilst you are also drawing on the energy from others. That is why it is very important to be in balance and look after your own energy.

The human energy field or the aura as it is known is made of several different layers, whilst each layer is connected to the chakra system.

There are several layers to the aura, which in turn are connected to the chakra system (energy centers, 7 major ones and loads of small ones) which are connected to the meridians (energy flowing path within the body).

The first layer of the aura is the Physical Layer which is closest to your body, and relates to your physical body, muscles, tissues and bones. It is weak when immunity is low or for people who don't exercise much, or are less active and it is stronger in people who are very active.

The second layer is the Emotional Layer, which represents emotions and feelings. It can be very affected in times of emotional stress.

The third layer is the Mental Layer which represents thoughts, mental ability and the state of your mind. It will be stronger in people who engage in mental tasks or have an overactive mind, and radiates the strongest when creativity is in flow.

If something emotional happens to us it will affect our emotional layer then this can lead into our emotional layer and our physical layer, thus affecting our chakras which are connected to these

layers and affecting the meridians which are connected to the chakras.
Example ; losing someone you love will have an effect on your mind, body and soul.

Something on a physical layer can lead out into the emotional and mental layers. Something traumatic happening to your body, say for example breaking a bone after falling off a bike, can have an effect on you mentally (making you afraid to ride a bike again) then this can lead out into the emotional layer.

When something affects us, no matter how big or small it might seem, it can create a domino effect and end up affecting us on many different levels, leading to unbalance in the body, mind and soul.

Each layer of the aura is a different colour, when we are balanced each layer is strong on its own, but when we are out of balance the layer that it is affecting may look sluggish, lighter or darker in colour, not as vibrant and may start seeping into the other layers.

Vibration and Frequency

All energy healing therapies work on a similar basic principle. We are energy beings, we have an aura or energy field which surrounds and includes our physical body. In a state of dis-ease (illness, stress, worry etc.), blocks will form in the aura and the energy flow will slow down.

From a schooling point of view, in physics we learn that matter is made up of molecules. Even something that is solid, such as a table, is vibrating all the time.

As humans, we are energy, we too are vibrating. When you say someone has "good vibes," you are really talking about that person's energy - happy people vibrate on a higher frequency. You can feel their energy. It is the same with unhappy or angry people, you can instantly feel the dense and low vibe that they are giving off.

Places have vibes too. When you walk into a room in which a fight has just occurred, you may feel a dense energy that makes you want to leave right away. Whereas when you are at the beach you can feel the clear, fresh and renewed energy.

GROUNDING

Grounding basically means being earthed.

Electricity is a form of energy so that has to be earthed in order for it to be safe to use. The same principle applies to us.

Grounding means to establish a feeling of self- awareness, a foundation of the consciousness of one's own self. In energy terms, it means to establish a connecting awareness in the unity of body, mind and spirit.

Grounding could be one of the most important and powerful personal awareness, health and healing practices for you to understand and apply in your daily life. Being grounded and having unity in body, mind and spirit is the beginning of becoming present, being whole and complete, having a life you love. It calls first for intending this reality for yourself, then it calls for awareness.

The process of waking up to yourself and your life is the process of becoming aware of what is really going on, not just what your stories, judgments and opinions are, then paying attention to your senses and perceptions, realizing the truth about your thoughts and thinking.

You must be grounded to be aware. You must have unity of body, mind and spirit to be present, whole and complete, to have a life you love.

A LITTLE ABOUT ME

Let me introduce myself. I was always the type of person that believed everyone should be treated equally and that no one person is better than another. Growing up I was a bit of a dreamer, I would be the one sitting in class, concentrating on turning the lights off with my eyes like I am one of the X-men, but I would settle for when they dimmed a little, even if I was just imagining it.

Even from a very young age, I had my own mind, and no one could tell me differently. This became more evident as I got older especially as I progressed into secondary school. In one of my school reports, the teacher changed the result for religion from satisfactory to "careless - indifferent approach to work" all because I had a different opinion to him.

I remember the topic was on this rape case referred to as Case X here in Ireland. A young girl was raped and became pregnant by the rapist. There was a big controversy whether she should be allowed to get an abortion.

I was 16 at the time, and my view was that this girl was entitled to do whatever she wanted to do, she did not ask to get raped, she did not ask to get pregnant, it should not be up to complete strangers, middle aged men and women or a 19th century law to decide her fate for her. The teacher did not like my opinion as he was all for her not getting an abortion, he was not used to students having and expressing their own opinions. It is not that I am for or against abortion, but I am for the health and well-being of every individual.

These classes were supposed to be open-minded and a debate style, where the students were encouraged to express their own opinions, but this was never going to happen in a religious school that was very much ruled by the Catholic Church.

I really struggled in secondary school. I could not find the right people to fit in with, I didn't know what I wanted to do, I didn't know what I liked or didn't like and I never really made proper friends. Now I know this was down to me sucking up everyone's energy and being really sensitive to everyone else's emotions. I absolutely hated it, but I didn't know what was going on and it wouldn't be until years later, actually only now when I am looking back on it, that I understand why I was the way I was.

I was not me because I actually wasn't me, I was everyone else, I was a sponge.

I always felt a lot of peer pressure as this school was very much sports orientated. My brother was a brilliant sports player so the pressure was being piled on me to be more like him, we were and still are totally different people, might I add the pressure was not by my parents or by him for that matter.

They were never like this, they were and are the best you could ask for. He would get very good grades whereas I did not really care about it. I was just dreamer, dreaming of travelling, dreaming of freedom, dreaming of getting out of this place and this time.

I went to an all boys school so the energy was very intense for me, especially after coming from being in a mixed primary school. The combination of just male energy was hard. I strived for the female energy so it turned out that I would go through numerous girlfriends but never really settling down and formed some really close friendships with a few girls, to which I still remain friendly with today.

I went from being a happy carefree child in primary to a depressed anxiety prone teenager turning to smoking, self-harm, drink and rebellious ways in a matter of weeks. I often skipped school, would go off to the city for myself, just wandering around, I would often sit down somewhere and just start writing something.

I had so much going on in my head, I would just sit and write whatever it was that had to come out. I found a big release in that.

When I was roughly 16, a small changed occurred when I found myself taking an overdose on prescription tablets. It was not really a cry for help, as I did not even know what I was doing, or what help I needed, but I never wanted to die, that was never an intention and it wasn't for attention either. I think I was just so spaced out of it, it was like I was possessed, and a spur of the moment action.

Before going into school one morning, I downed roughly fifty tablets which should have been enough to knock out a horse. I remember going into a free German class and being totally out of it, coming back in and out of consciousness whilst still being there.

I went to the bathroom, had a smoke and phoned my parent's friend who collected me, he took me to their house and I went to bed for the day as well as a trip to the hospital. Of course, the stories that followed afterwards were a little bit more exaggerated, supposedly I puked all over the bathrooms, I had to be carried out of the school, I was dead, my stomach was pumped, etc.

Note; my stomach was not pumped, I would reckon there was no need to with the amount I puked.

This was a turning point for me, but it was still going to be a few years before I eventually found my way back to who I was and to who I was supposed to become.

Everyday going into school was hard, I struggled with the thought of it. The school principle and I never ever saw eye-to-eye. On the day I was receiving my leaving certificate results, he had to have one last dig at me and called me into his office to receive them. Then he proceeded to give me one last lecture with a disgusted look in his eyes of what he thought of me, before telling me that no matter what I do in my life I will always need him as a reference on my CV.

I smiled the most genuine heartfelt smile I ever did in all my life walking out those gates for what would be my last time under his control. I felt relief, I felt happy and I knew that I would never have to have anything to do with him ever again. I felt like I was being released from jail, heading right into my freedom. Amazingly I never put his name on any applications or CV's that I used, and I was never asked either.

Whilst he will look back and see a version of me that he sees through his eyes and what he wants to believe I was, I can always look back and besides the hard times I struggled with personally in his establishment, I will look back on those years of learning who I was, how to treat people and realise how much I had yet to learn.

He may look at me with disgust but I will look back at the younger me who helped so many people back then, which he never even realised or would have even considered I was capable of doing, even though I was struggling myself.

I will remember the friend who became pregnant and I took her hand to ensure her that everything will be alright.

I will remember the friends whose brother committed suicide and I was there for them whenever they needed me, I went out of my way to make sure that they had someone to lean on.

I will remember all the people who were being bullied that I resolved the issues for.

I will remember how I talked people out of doing some very foolish things.

I will remember how I was there for people when their loved ones passed away.

I will remember how I comforted people when their relationships ended.

One thing that I can gaurentee that I will never forget is the look he gave me and the last words that he said to me, that was the look and the words that I needed to hear for me to realise that my time is here and my time is now.

When I say I will not forget his words, I do not mean that I will remember them in spite or in vengeance or that I am holding a grudge, as I am not. I will remember those words for how they showed me how much I grew and had so much more to learn. I will remember those words, his tone and the glaring look for how they set me free, teaching me how to treat people. I will remember those words for showing me what I never want to be.

Looking back, I know I was not there for the academics, I was there to learn about life, preparing me for the future. I was there to learn about me, not about history.

Realistically, I can totally understand from a certain point his actions towards me, he grew up in a different time and had completely different beliefs and opinions than I had, if I had to put up with the version of me that he had to, without knowing or even apprehending to question why I was the way I was, I probably would of treated me like that too and would of breathed a sigh of relief when I walked out of the office.
We were from two totally separate generations, he grew up in a society that no longer existed, an era that was coming to an end whilst I was growing up in a society that was forever changing.

The start of the journey home

This is probably the most important sign that I have ever received because if I hadn't, I would not be sitting here writing this after learning everything that I have and, on the path, to rediscovering myself, or as I like to call it - coming home.

I was away on a stag weekend and my father said that he would collect me on the Sunday. For some unknown reason to me at the time, I rang my father on the Saturday and asked him to collect me early on the Sunday morning, as in 8.30/9am, the earlier the better.

Anyone that knew me back then would know that on a weekend, especially if I am drinking, there is not a hope that I would of been up before midday (I would have been lucky to be comings home at that time). My mother and brother were telling him that there is no way that I would be up, not to mind even be ready to come home. My father stuck to his guns, he knew that I would, he knew there was something going on and knew how adamant I was that I would be ready.

I remember leaving the hotel at 8am in the morning, and waiting outside for him until he arrived around 845am.
He asked how come I wanted to come home so early and I said I just wanted to get out of there for some reason, that something

was up and I had a voice in my head since the day before telling me that I had to get home.

When we reached the outskirts of the town I got a text telling me that my friend was after dying the night before.

So, looking back on it now and putting the pieces together, it would have been a lot harder on me if I was not on my way home or with my father when I found this out. This is the message that I received that started me on the path to recovery and discovery.

I, obviously at that stage in my life could not understand what had happened for me to make the phone call to come home early, but I was determined to find out. I did not know who or what was the voice in my head, but I knew that when I did not take notice of it, it got louder and when I listened I just knew to do what it was telling me to do. It felt right.

Looking back on it now, for the whole weekend away, I stuck to myself, and did my own thing. Everyone else went off doing activities, but I was quite happy to go do my own thing. I know a lot was going on in my own life at the time, and I needed the space to myself to unpack what was happening. At various stages throughout the day I could hear the voice in my head and

I kept putting it down to myself just thinking random thoughts. I was not in a very good place mentally but it was as the day went on and the more I dismissed it, the louder and clearer the message became. I had to come home, not just to my physical home but I had to start coming back home to me, to who I naturally was and who I am meant to become.

I had been so lost for many years, not knowing where I stood in life, what I was meant to do or what my passions were. This weekend was the weekend that I truly decided to start living, it opened my eyes to a world that I shut out for so long.

The voice I was hearing inside my head was a voice that I was very familiar with, a one that was always there for me and always put me on the right path, but it was a voice I didn't fully know or trust yet.

Welcome to

The Energy Sessions

THE ENERGY SESSIONS consist of the messages that I have received. It can be read in one go or on days that you are not feeling the best, you can just randomly pick a page and see what it means to you.

These sessions have the potential to give you the key to unlock all the chains that you have been tied to - physically, mentally, emotional and spiritually, helping you to unchain to the rhythm of the world that you have become so accustomed to, to live your best life, the life that you truly deserve, if you choose to.

These sessions will give you the ability to break free from all that you think that you are, giving you the freedom to take back your own power, owning who you are and embracing what the future holds for you, knowing without a shred of doubt that everything will be ok.

The one thing in life that we are guaranteed is the one thing that we fear.

Is it not a bit ironic that the one thing in life that we are guaranteed is the one thing that most of us are afraid of?

From the first breath that we take, we start this journey so maybe it is actually living is what we are truly afraid of.

People hang onto money like they can take it with them, but there ain't no hitch on a hearse.

People hold on to grudges but what is the point?
It does not make you feel good.

People try to hang on to power, but there will not be a twenty foot box especially for your ego.

We are always living our lives wanting, wanting and wanting more, that we tend to forget what we have and what truly matters.

The one thing in life that we are guaranteed is what we fear but the one thing we can do, is choose to live.

Do you choose to live your life in fear?

Do you choose to live your life in regret?

Do you choose to live your life to please everyone else but yourself?

Is arguing, fighting or holding grudges really worth your attention or energy in the grand scheme of things?

If there is something you want to do, why not take the chance and do it? The worst thing that can happen is, it does not work out.

If there is something you want to say, just say it.
The worst thing that can happen is that you do not hear back what you wanted to hear, but you will never know if you do not speak up.

One thing you do not want to do is to look back on your life with the "I should have done this, said that or went there".

Stop fearing and start living.

Every morning you wake up is not just a good day,
it is a great day.

Every day that you get to see the sun rise is a blessing.

Everyone in your life will have a last day with you
and you never know when it will be
but what you can do is to be sure that
the last words that you speak are always good
and not words that you will live to regret.

27375

Let's talk numbers and depending where you are, give or take a few hundred.

So, this is the average daily lifespan of a person in the United States - 27375.

When you add a few hundred it does not really make it seem that much more in the grand scheme of things.

Twenty-Seven Thousand, Three Hundred and Seventy-Five!!!!

That is what we have if we are lucky and that is actually including all the hours and minutes that we spend sleeping, eating, working, in school, etc.

Two-Seven-Three-Seven-Five
It is not really that much when you think of it that way, so please do not waste it.....

Try to make memories every day and try to remember the moments, for they are what will get us through a bad day.

We always remember the days where something tragic or something significant happens and how we felt at the time but imagine if we started to remember every day that we have, every single moment that makes us feel good.

How many days do we waste worrying about insignificant things?

How many hours have we wasted on things or on people that simply do not matter?

We spend so much of our time preoccupied with things that really do not matter, people who do not matter to us, doing jobs that we actually despise and holding grudges that are doing us no good.

Try to do something every day that pleases you.
Remember every morning that you wake up is a new opportunity, a new opportunity for you to either seize the day or let the day seize you.

One thing that you should always remember is that there are so many people who would love to be where you are right now.

No matter what is going on in the world or in your life, do not let it dim your light, all you have to do is flip the switch and appreciate everything that you have and all that you are.

Two-Seven-Three-Seven-Five

"27,375"

Who Am I?

Who am I?

What is real?

Who is the you that never changes?

We are in many bodies since the day we were born, we are constantly changing.

Your body is not real but you believe that it is.

Your body is not who you are.

What is real does not change.

Who you are does not occupy your body.

You can search for your 20 year old body and I can guarantee you that, you will never find it.

Who we are is not what we have.

Who we are is not what we do.

Who we are is not what other people think of us.

Face of a son,

Face of a father,

Face of a brother,

Face of a friend,

Face of a co-worker,

who knows the struggles within.

In any given moment, we are a number of different people to another person. What they perceive us to be can be alluding to who we actually are.

First and foremost, I am a father, it is the proudest person I will ever be, knowing that I created this amazing human being who is growing up and becoming himself, knowing that I am a part of his DNA and that no matter what I will be with him forever.

We are all connected, as I am connected to him, my parents are connected to him, the thousands of ancestors that lie behind us are still here and connected to us.

If it wasn't for the love of thousands
we would cease to exist.

It is a magnificent cycle, we are all energy and since energy never dies, they are still here with us, inside us, helping us, within our hearts. They are here with us at any given moment in time.

People label for familiarity

To one person I am a brother

To two people I am a son

To one person I am a father

To a few I am a friend

To the stranger in the street I am no body

To work I am just a number

I am a cousin

I am a nephew

I am me

Whilst all these labels are true

I am all but none

I am what I am I am

But the most important question is

Who am I to me?

Look Beyond

In relation to anyone in your life, or any person that you know or you may come across on the street, you will only ever see the face that they decide to show you, not the heart that lies within, or the struggles that they face, all their hardships or their embraces.

We really do not know anyone, we really do not know what is happening in anyone's life, we do not know what goes on behind closed doors, we do not know the trials and tribulations that anyone faces.

We only ever really know someone from what they want us to know about them and from our own perceptions and our personal relationships with the person.

This is true for every single person that you know and that is in your life.

As hard as this is to believe, your parents actually had a life before you existed.
Your partners had a life before you met.
Your children will have a life to live after you are gone.

All these people also have a life and so many different relationships that does not and should not involve you.

You are only ever a percentage of someone's life.
I am not saying this in a bad way, but what I mean is that you need to live a life separate to everyone else, you need to live your life for you.

Every relationship that you have in your life is different and individual.

You will have a different relationship with your mother than you have with your father.

Your parents will have different relationships to your siblings than the relationship that they have with you.

You will have a different relationship with your brother than the relationship you have with your friends.

You will have a different relationship to your kids than the relationship you have with your partner.

Your partners relationships with your kids will be different to your relationships with your kids.

You should never feel let down or judge someone by something that they did in a life before you existed to them or that has nothing at all to do with you.

If it happened before your relationship with them, it has nothing to do with your relationship with them.

If it has nothing to do with your relationship with them, it has nothing to do with you.

You are only ever responsible for your personal relationships with others, not their relationships with everyone else or for a matter of fact their relationship towards you.

START ROMANTICISING YOUR LIFE

Believing in yourself is never easy and is challenging at the best of times but when you push through all of your fears and boundaries, what if it is all worth it in the end, when you reach the other side?

So, step out of your comfort zone, and push through your boundaries, the chances are it is always sunnier on the other side.

If you have a dream, it is there for a reason, that is to make it a reality. If you have a passion that you love doing, the only thing stopping you from doing it is your mind.

Would you rather live your life in regret
and never know?
OR
Would you rather take the chance and
learn along the way?

If you know and feel something that is right for you, you will know what you need to do, without even thinking about it, no matter what obstacles are in the way you will just jump over them.

You know that feeling of being on a high where everything just feels so good and right, there is a beat in your body, there is a skip to your step, that is the feeling that you need to keep.

People will try to bring you down, they will try to knock what you have planned, they will try to put doubt inside your mind, and at times it will hurt but this is the test you got to take to prove to you what is right.

Block out their fear, and stand in your own power.
Do not let the fears or the insecurities of others become yours.

Generally, the people we love mean well, but act from their own fears and insecurities, so do not confuse their fears, their insecurities and the limitations that they put on themselves as yours.

Too many times we hear of people on their death bed, wishing that they should have said this or did that, realise from this day forth that you have a choice, do not choose to be one of these people.

You should not be taking your last few breaths still dreaming of what you never got to do or what you should have said, you want to take those breaths thinking of the memories that you made, the love that you had and the people that truly mattered.

So, start romanticising your life, start thinking of yourself as the main character in your own movie,
the one that you root for, the one that gets the girl,
the job, the car, the house, the holiday.

You have got to root for yourself, like you root for everyone else.
You have got to start believing in yourself without a shred of doubt.
Dream big, enjoy and learn from every step along the way.

Everyone wants the fairytale ending, but not everyone even believes that they can have it or believes that they deserve it.
When you choose to become the writer of your own story (destiny) and stop putting the control (power) in someone else's hands, every dream that you have, can and will become a reality.

Do not live your life in regret and do not believe that you are too old, do not believe that you are too under qualified or not good enough to achieve whatever it is that you want.

You deserve the best and do not let anyone tell you otherwise.

Are you alive or are you just breathing?

It is ok at the moment to just be breathing, to be just surviving but do not let this rule your life going forward.

Every day we breathe but not every day can we actually say that we are alive.

Ask yourself the following questions.
What is your passion?
What is it that brings you to life?
What can you do that makes you feel alive?

You do not want to just spend your life merely just in existence, you want to live.

You need to feel that fire in your belly, the freedom of the wind blowing with you as you fall through the air, the exhilaration of that first touch, that is how you need to be if You want to feel alive.

Pursue the things that push you creatively but are like second nature for you to do. That is where your passion lies, that is what you are meant to do.

Never settle for what does not fuel your fire in all manners of life, relationships, family, work.

With every decision that you will have to make from this day forward, ask yourself will it bring you to life or will you just simply be breathing?

We have to breathe to survive but
we have to be alive to thrive.

They say I should

They say I should do this.

They say I should do that.

They say I should not say this.

They say I should say that.

They say my beliefs are wrong.

They say I should think like them.

They say that I should do what they want me to do.

The list goes on and on.

This is the society that we live in, people are too scared to be themselves over what other people will think of them.

But the real questions are ;

Who are they to tell you how to live your life?
What gives anyone else the right to tell you how to live your life?
Who made them God?
Are you going to let them have control over your life, your plans and your dreams?

OR

Are you going to take back your power and be unique by being you, living your life in the way that makes you happy?

Forget about everyone else, what they do, what they think, at the end of the day this is your life, live it the way you want to live it, do not be dictated to or feel like you should live your life for someone else.

Do not live your life the way others want and think you should live it.

YOU HAVE A CHOICE IN EVERY SINGLE THING

<u>You choose ;</u>

Your thoughts.

Your opinions.

Your battles.

Your perceptions.

<u>You choose ;</u>

How you react.

How you feel.

How you respond.

How you get back up.

<u>You choose ;</u>

Where you direct your attention.

If you are going to let other people and situations affect you.

How you let other people treat and talk to you.

What you learn from every experience, situation and relationship that you have.

<u>You choose ;</u>

The level of respect and love you receive from anyone based on how much you love and respect yourself.

You have to do for you what you would do for others. Self-care is not a necessity, it is a priority. Choosing to put you first is not selfish, it is the choice to love and respect yourself, the one person that you spend the most time with.

The relationship you have with yourself is the single most important relationship that you will ever have, which means it is the most important relationship that you will ever have the pleasure to work on and nourish.

SWEETER IS THE GLORY

More people want you to fail than actually want to see you succeed. Some people might want you to do good but the majority of them will not want you to do better than them.

I want you to read that paragraph again, but this time really read it and let it sink in.

More people want you to fail than actually want to see you succeed. Some people might want you to do good but the majority of them will not want you to do better than them.

Do not leave them, their beliefs or criticisms get in your way, remember that you were born to thrive, you were born to fly, do not be bound to other people's chains.

They will tell you that you cannot do that, but what if you can? They will tell you that it will never work out for you, but what if it does?
You will never know unless you try.

Do not let anything hold you back,
especially your mind.

You have got to believe in yourself without a shred of doubt and you must not take any notice of what anyone else says, does or thinks.

You have got to believe it and believe in yourself before you can achieve it.

You do not need anyone in your life who will put you down. Why would you even acknowledge someone or let them have a say in how you live your life, especially if their best intentions are not for you to succeed?

You are worth far more than that and there are plenty of other people who will believe in you and want you to succeed. There are plenty of other people who will believe in you but your paths have just not yet crossed.

Remember that life and time is precious, you can never get it back once it's gone so make sure that you choose to live your life and spend your time the way you want to. Live your life for you, not for anybody else.

Confine to the norms they say

Confine to the norms they say, now I realise that there is no such thing as normal. What is "normal" just does not suit me anymore.

I gave in to peer pressure, I went and had a few (too many) drinks. I could blame the people that I was with and say that they made me do it, but the real answer was I made myself do it. People that I used to be friendly with would come home for a weekend expecting me to give up my time, to meet up with them and do what they want.

What is actually wrong here is that, I really do not enjoy being in their company, but yet I felt obliged to be in their company. I felt like I had to meet up with them, I felt like I had to drink whilst I was in their company because otherwise I would not be able to stick them for the night.

I should have realised when I felt like I would have to drink whilst in their company, that says it all really, I knew that I did not want to but I felt that I had to.

What I forgot at the time was that I do not have to do anything to make anyone else happy or to do anything that I do not want to. I decided to buy a box of cigarettes, I knew I was going to be spending the night in the smoking room, listening to stories that I have no interest in, and they do not really want my opinion anyway, so I will revert back to the old me, just for tonight, the fella that would sit, drink, listen, smoke and let you think that you know me, while I continue to drink so I am oblivious to what you are saying to me. It does not matter if I want to tell them what I think, because they are the cool radical people who travel the world, to them I am merely just the single parent working the full-time job I have had for years, with no prospects.

I may have been that single parent that was working the same job for years, but that job paid me money so I could be at home with my child, we got to go on our holidays, it was a job that suited me at that time without having to uproot my whole life, I was able to give my child the best possible life that I could at that time, I know that the best thing in the world is love, I have and give that every single second of the day.

I knew I did not want to go out, I am quite happy at home of a Saturday night, watching a movie and knowing that I will not have a sick head or be too tired on a Sunday morning to simply be even just present with my kid or to get up in the morning, go to the gym and bring home the hot chocolate and pancakes.

That is me now, I am happy. I do not need anyone's approval of what I like or what I am into, I have my dreams and my hopes, the only one that can quash them is me.

The lesson I learned is that, sometimes you have to leave old friends in the past, they can still be stuck as the person they were five, ten even twenty years ago and I am not that person anymore, no matter how I try to be. I do not even know why I tried to be him again, I do not even like him, I like who I am now, who I am becoming and I will never allow myself to change for anyone ever again, even if it is just for a mere 5 hours of a Saturday night.

To the old me, goodbye.
To me now, welcome home.

We have to acknowledge ourselves

We have to acknowledge who we are and make the most of what we have got, that is when we will truly come into the person that we are meant to be.

We all have desires, we all have dreams, we all have hopes and we all have fears that either pull us back or push us forward.

Once we own our desires, our dreams, our hopes and our fears, we will own ourselves, and no one will ever be able to take away who you are, from you again.
Once the mask comes off we find out who the true being is.

People have this illusion that being "spiritual" is that you are zen all the time, that nothing ever affects you and nothing will ever anger you, but that is not being spiritual, that is being totally unrealistic.

Spiritual to me is about being in touch with your higher self, your emotions, your thoughts, your inner being, with everyone else, all that came before us and all that will come long after we are gone. Being spiritual is acknowledging every emotion and realising that we are still human.

You cannot be spiritual without being human.
Being human is all about the emotions - love, anger, happiness, sadness.

Why deny these feelings and suppress them?
That is not why we are here and it is definitely not what we are here to do. When in spirit we will live like that, never having to worry about anything we are feeling, thinking, saying or doing.

Whilst we are human, we all have a time limit, so enjoy every moment, if you feel angry do not beat yourself up over it. You are allowed to have all these feelings and emotions, it is normal, it is being human, it is a feeling of being alive.

No-one determines your happiness, not I or any self-help book can tell you what is right for you.

Only you yourself know what is right for you.

OUT WITH THE OLD

As you change, which is inevitable by the way, all the people around you will change as well. Some people are just like energy vampires and drain all your energy, it can take you days even possibly weeks to get over it but if you protect yourself these people cannot attack your energy and bring you down.

Old friends are a great example of this, they might annoy you, irritate you, talk down to you, etc.

Why should you put up with it?
If you only speak to them two or three times a year, and this is how you feel after being in their company, do you honestly think that you should be with them?

Ask yourself the following questions:
How do you survive the rest of your time without them?
Why can you survive the rest of your time without them?
Did you feel better with or without being in their company?
Why not cut them out of your life?
What is stopping you?

The only person that is stopping you doing this is YOU.

Having ties to the past you,
will serve the current you no good.

Think about it this way -

You have changed, they have changed, holding onto memories of the past times you have shared together is pointless, when you can be making new memories now, with people on the same level as you.

Do not feel obligated to anyone, or to do anything, if it does not feel right to you.

Just because you used to hang out when you were teenagers, you used to socialise at weekends in your twenties, or that your families are life long friends, you are not obliged to do it now, you are not obliged to them or to anyone else for that matter, the only person you are obliged to is yourself.

Think about the words "used to", it is in the past.
As painful and as challenging as that can be at times, sometimes people and things are better off left in the past.

They serve you no purpose now, this is your life, so all you want in your life is people and things that make you feel good, make you happy and are good for you NOW.

People come into your life for a reason,
a season or a lifetime.

LET THEM GO

We will all lose friends over the way we are developing, evolving or dare I say changing. It might be hard to understand and you might never understand it.

We all change and when we change we may not be going in the same direction that others in our lives want us to go in or they might not like the way we have changed but do not take any of it personally.

The ones that are meant for you will stick with you, the ones that do not stick with you are the ones that you were meant to shed. They are not your tribe. You can reach out and try clinging to who you were in order to keep them in your life, but do you really want them to want you for who you were rather than who you are now, what you have become or who you are becoming?

Who you are becoming is far more important than who you ever were.

Self-Talk is Contagious

Do not let your first thought in the morning be full of negativity. Your first thought in the morning sets your mood and your tone for the rest of your day, and it is very hard to change it around as the day goes on. Everyday you wake up is your day and you decide how it goes in those first few seconds, not anyone else.

Start to pay more attention to how you start your day and pay attention to how your day unfolds with how you choose to start it.

I am not one of these people for positive mantras and the glitz that goes with them, do not get me wrong I love positive quotes that strike a meaning but I am not a person who will endlessly repeat them in my head, to me you will only be repeating words written by someone else and the majority of the time you do not even know what you are saying and it can become so repetitive that it is mundane and has no meaning or effect. Find and write your own mantras, ones that resonate with you, how you want to be and how you want to feel.

You need to feel what you say, do and think.

What I am is a person who is extra mindful of the way
I talk to myself.

Yes, I have the times I am like "ugh for F*** sake" and beat myself up for a while over stuff but I try to be extra mindful of the way I do talk to myself.

Our bodies listen to every single thing that we feed it.
By saying I am sick, I do not feel good, I am tired - surprise surprise, that is how I end up feeling,

I am sick, I am sick - results in you starting to feel sick.
I am tired, I am tired - results in you feeling tired.
I cannot do that - results in "shock, horror" you do not even try to do it.

Telling yourself that you are no good at something results in you telling yourself that you will never be good at it, which inevitably means you will not be good at it.

We all know the story of the two wolves and the boy asking his grandfather which one will win, and the grandfather says the one that you feed is the one who succeeds. Think about it, if you are constantly going around talking negatively to yourself, your body and energy is going to respond to what it is listening to.

You are either building yourself up or tearing yourself down with every single thought that you have.

Think about it, with every single thought that you have, You alone are either building yourself up or tearing yourself down and setting limitations on You.

If you do not try something, how do you know you cannot do it??
Why limit yourself without even trying?
Worst possible scenario - you cannot do it and you learn from trying.

Every thought, every feeling and every single word has energy.
Negative thoughts plus negative words equals negative outcome.
Positive thoughts plus positive words equals positive outcome.
A negative scenario, no matter what it is, will always be overcome by a positive feeling or thought.

Your thoughts can completely change your day, but make sure that they change it for the better.

Pay attention to the way that you talk to yourself.
You will talk to yourself more than you will ever talk to anybody else, the single most important relationship you will ever have is with yourself.

Why be self critical?
If you allow yourself to treat yourself that way, criticising yourself, belittling yourself, why are you then so shocked when someone else treats you that way?

Choose what substance you want to feed your mind, it is the same as choosing what food you want for your body to be strong, healthy, lean, etc. When you feed your mind with good nourishing thoughts, those will shine through your body.

Your relationship with yourself determines everyone else's relationship towards you.

Think about it, every single relationship you have in your life will always be based on your relationship with yourself.

YOU ARE IN CHARGE OF YOUR LIFE

This is your life so take responsibility for it, do not take it for granted and do not take it too seriously.

You are in charge of your life, absolutely no one else has the power to control your life unless you give them the power.

People will always try to tell you what way to live your life, the way that they think you should live it, the way they want you to, the way that they live theirs.
They want you to live your life the way they want, to make them feel comfortable.

What gives them the right to tell you the way you should live Your Life?

Living is meant to be fun, it is about having new experiences and learning. It is about enjoying yourself, loving yourself and loving others.

So get out there and try something new. Do not get stuck in a box, doing the same routine every day, do something that excites you and makes you feel good.

Obstacles cannot stop you.

People cannot stop you.

Only You can stop You.

We all make mistakes, but we must not leave our mistakes define us, we must learn from them and move on. Realistically there is actually no such thing as a mistake, they are only lessons that we learn along the way.

There is nothing wrong with starting again tomorrow, once every other day does not become like today.

We divide everything up into time, when we should really be living in the now.

Yesterday is gone and tomorrow does not exist. Believe it or not but you cannot do anything about the past, you should just leave the future come when it does and enjoy what you have right now.

Appreciate every single thing that you have and live in the present moment. There is a reason it is called the present, there is no other time but now.

Live your life how you want to.

Do not let other people's moods affect yours

Do you know that some people just want to be grumpy and bring other people down?
Do you realise that this is because they are just not happy in themselves?

They dislike seeing other people happy and getting on with their lives. They do not like you having a life, having friends, doing and having what you want. They leave their bitterness build up and take it out on everybody else.

The only people they care about are themselves, and ironically with attitudes like theirs, they actually do not even care about themselves, because they are neglecting themselves with their own behaviour.

My response to people like this is "f**k them", apologies for the language but it really is the best response, it is their issues to be dealing with not yours.

No one has the right to make others feel bad just because they feel it.

Why should your day be screwed up over other people's issues? The answer is it should not..

Why should your mood change just because of other people's attitude? The answer is it should not.

So do not leave people like this bring you down to their level, that is what they want, they want you to be as miserable and just as bitter as they are.

You deserve the best, do not let anyone tell you any different.

Do not take the bait, if someone tries to pick an argument with you, have the power to walk away. You are probably just the easiest person for them to fight with, so trust yourself not to stoop to their level, leave them work through their own problems, their own issues, it belongs to them not you, so do not take it on, and don't take it personally.

You do not have to or need to carry a dead weight up a mountain.

CHANGE YOUR THOUGHTS TO CHANGE YOUR LIFE

The way we look at things is usually by the way we were taught to see by other people, it is the way we were conditioned and are still being conditioned to this day, until we realise that we have the power inside of us to think for ourselves, to gather our own opinions and to make up our own minds.

The majority of the time we look through our eyes and our thoughts, which ironically are not even our thoughts, it is seeing what you were told to look at and see, but it is not often that we are told or for that matter that we were even taught how to feel with our hearts.

When you look and feel through your heart, everything is so much more clearer, it makes sense.

Did you ever stop and think -
Why you do not like a particular person?
Why you do not like a particular food?
Why you do not like a particular place?

The simple answer could be that it reminded you of something you were told was not good for you, something you were told was too dangerous to go near, someone who got you in trouble when you were young.

You have stuck to these beliefs and have not developed your own. You might have been given out to for expressing your beliefs and desires, that way you bottled them up and fed other people's beliefs into your system, in order to fit in and not to be different.

The fear of being different, the fear of standing up for what you think is right, the fear of the outcome if you do express yourself, the fear of repercussions, the fear of being ridiculed and mocked.

It is these fears that make us bury our heads in the sand and forget what we personally think. We then stop our own individual development and listen to what other people tell us, like teachers, peers, friends and parents. It is not their fault either because it is an endless cycle and that is the way they were taught to believe.

The fear of leaving a job, because you were told that it is hard to get a job these days, so you stick with this job even though you despise it but you get your wage at the end of the week.

These thought forms are scary, but do not leave them rule your life.

Why should you live your life based on other people's beliefs?

Why should you not pursue what you want because of what other people think?

Who says that it will not work out for you?

Why do you think it is ok not to do what you want?

Why do you leave yourself "think" that you believe what they are saying?

Why believe that you are not capable of all that you desire and deserve?

Why do you think you do not deserve the best?

Change the way you think about things and change your life.

Start feeling and sensing with your heart rather than looking and thinking with your eyes and with your mind.

We were not born this way, it is the way that society makes us conform, so we do not actually know any other way to be or to think the majority of the time but once you learn to shut off the mind and start listening to your heart and feelings, everything becomes so much easier and clearer, resulting in your life becoming so much better in the process.

YOUR OUTLOOK WILL BE THE OUTCOME

You will always be given a challenge, no matter how good your life is going, no matter how much you want something, even if everything is going smoothly, you will always have another hurdle to over come.

You can be doing what you love, you can be with the one person that you are destined to be with, but there will always be times of stress and sorrow.

Sorry to tell you but you are not going to find all the answers at the top of the mountain. Everything takes work, and it is continuous, once you reach the top of one mountain, another one will appear, but with each step the climb will get easier.

No matter how far you have come, there will always be obstacles, that is life. How you conquer them depends on how you perceive them.

If you are going to face something with a pessimistic view, then there should be no shocks when you get hit ten times fold, whereas when you face it head on full of optimism, then the battle is halved.

You can have everything in the world, all the riches that you may have dreamed of but what is the point if you do not have anyone to share it with?

We spend so much time worried about what everyone else has, that we never actually count our own blessings and appreciate what we have ourselves. There are plenty of people who would be happy and grateful to be in your shoes.

You will never be able to reach what is in front of you until you let go of what is behind you.

Quality over Quantity

We all should and we all need to live our lives focusing on the quality that we have, rather than the quantity that we want or think that we may need.

You can have hundreds of friends, but maybe only one real good one and that is the one that truly matters.

People think that we need more of everything, that we need more friends, that we need more money, that we need more likes, we need more followers, that we need more possessions to be happy, but it could be only one thing that really makes the difference for us.

You could spend hours reading a book that is 400 pages long but just because it is bigger does not make it better than the book that is 40 pages long. You could get so much more out of the 40 pages than out of the entire 400 pages.

The only thing in this life that we need more of is love.

LIFE'S PURPOSE

I used to think that life needed a purpose but now I know that, you give your life purpose.

What you do, what you think, what you can bring into this world is what gives your life purpose and meaning.

What you think is what you create. So, think about all the good things that have happened to you, now think how did you feel when they happened.

We all have the misunderstanding that we cannot achieve everything we want, but in fact you can.

All you have to do is believe, have faith, have trust and persist. Never stop dreaming, your dreams are what you crave and what will make you happy. Your dreams are here for a reason, that is to give you hope and life.

Never give up faith, if you do not believe in yourself, how can you possibly expect someone else to believe in you?

Trust that you are on the right path, and even if you aren't, there will always be a crossroads where you can always veer off in the right direction.

There is always a way and means around everything. There is a force inside of you, that needs your belief to become real.

Look at life like a sat nav, it might not always be right or take you exactly where you want to go, it might take you the roundabout way, sometimes it can be dangerous, you have to update it every so often, but it will take you on a journey, a journey that may be far better than just sitting into your car and going straight where you thought you wanted to go.

What or who is meant for you will always find you, no matter what obstacle is in the way, if it is meant to be, it will be.

The road we take can veer left or right, circle right around, come to a halt or go full throttle, that is the life we live, but what is for us will not pass us, life is too short to get stuck in all the trials and tribulations.

It can be over in the blink of an eye, done and dusted, so why worry about things that you cannot control or that has nothing at all to do with you?

The moment you laugh
at the obstacles that life throws at you,
you are halfway through solving them.

LIFE CAN THROW YOU LEMONS BUT WHAT YOU ACTUALLY WANT IS GRAPES

It is the smaller things in life that we should appreciate more. Yes, you can have the big house, the fancy car, the fancy job but that will not guarantee to make you happy?

It is the simple things like waking up next to someone you love everyday that counts, the child that runs into your arms when you come home from a stressful day at work, (even when that child has their foot in your face at 3am in the morning), the dog that wags her tail and jumps about manically anytime she sees you, the smell of the freshly cut grass, the warmth of the sun upon your back, those first few drops of rain on your face.

These are all the simple things that anyone needs to make them happy. Do not get too caught up in what everyone else has or does, believe it or not but they are probably caught up on what other people have or does.

How much of what other people show you is actually real?

They might have that mansion and the fancy cars with all the trimmings but they could be crippled with debts, that sun holiday that they are smiling on and posting picture perfect images on social media could be costing them an arm and a leg which could be taking them years to pay off.

The crisp clean images around the family table could be and most likely are, hiding a completely different reality to what they are portraying.

LIFE CAN BE CRUEL

Sometimes life's lessons can be cruel, but what we all tend to forget is that it is the lessons in life that we learn and these obstacles that we face are what makes us who we are, and show us how to deal with all the different types of situations that we will be faced with down the line.

If we were not shown the bad things, we would not know what good things are, if we did not go through bad times, we would not know or appreciate the good times. Everything that we experience is giving us the opportunity to grow.

We just have to embrace every given moment, make the most of what we have and know that we are in charge of our own lives so we can change it all at any given moment.

If you wake up and are just in a bad mood, ask yourself is this the way you want your day to go?

Do not be defined by one bad start, change the way you think and change the way you look at things. Change your perspective and flip the switch.

All our power comes from our hearts, it is love that will change everything. If you are in a bad situation, or other people are bringing you down to their level, just think -

This is me,
This is my life,
These are my feelings,
I am in charge of how my day goes,
I am in charge of my feelings,
I am in charge of me,
This is my life,
This is me.

Remember to centre yourself, and picture the one thing that you love more than anything in this world and no one will come through that fortress, love is the answer and as cliché as this sounds, love is the key.

DO NOT LET FEAR OR DREAD GET IN YOUR WAY

We all have a habit of thinking what if this happens or how would I cope?

The truth is we do not know how we will cope or what we would do in any given situation, the only thing you can do is stop worrying about it. By worrying about something you are only setting yourself up for a fall.

If it has not happened yet, why worry about it now? Look at all the time you are wasting when you could be enjoying what you have. It is when we face obstacles that we truly know who we are and what we are capable of doing or becoming. We never know how we will respond or what we will do in any situation until it happens.

We never wish the best for ourselves, and why is that? We deserve happiness, we deserve love, we deserve money just as much as the next person.

Why would you limit yourself? Where you are in your life right now, might not be where you want to be, but it might be necessary for you to be there at this moment in time.

Be careful of what you tolerate as you are teaching people how to treat you.

From my own point of view, I had spent years working in a job that I really did not care about, but I was good at it and I will not lie, I also got stuck in a rut. As time went on, the more and more I stopped caring about it, but I had a child and also had bills to pay, so I could not just up and leave.

Even though I applied for numerous other jobs, I would never get them even though my cv was pretty good, it was disheartening at times, but there are reasons for everything. Ultimately, I half knew where or what I should be doing, I tried the normal college courses but they still did not ignite any flame in me, so I opted to train in numerous holistic courses and this is where I discovered my passion.

It was when Covid hit and the business that I was working in closed that I really discovered who I was without that place, I would meet people in the street asking me or telling me about my current employment status, that the job was gone, it was being leased out, it was never opening again, etc. All these people knew my status before I did but I was care free, a bit too much for a lot of people but for the first time in my life I felt free.

I was free from everyone and every tie I had since I was a child. It was testament to me that if I felt this good, this is what I had to be doing. It was not even that I was doing anything as I wasn't, but I was not there, I was gone, and I was coming back into who I was meant to be, I was on the way to doing what I am meant to be doing, I was free from being the me associated with that employment, those people and the place, I could finally be who I was meant to be.

Sure, I would have the days where people would get into my head telling me what I should be doing, that I cannot do this or rely on that for a living, but I would just have to bring myself back to me and see how I was feeling.

Every course, every conversation, every class that I ever gave or went to, was leading me to here. This was my crossroads that I finally got to choose which road to take, all by myself. When I stood back and looked at everything I did the previous few years, I knew I would be and will be grand, I was being shown what I can do and what I am capable of doing, all I have to do is believe in myself and trust that everything will unfold as it is meant to. I had to choose to trust my own words and advice, choose to not let anyone dim my light, quash my dreams or get inside my head.

After spending years working in a place, the respect that was shown to me was zero, I went 6 months without receiving a phone call or information regarding my employment from the employer, everyone else was told what my employment status was before I was told, I had to request documents and money that was owed to me, when I asked for my entitlements the phone was hung up on me, solicitors and barristers were involved on their behalf, the blame was being placed on me for the place not reopening. I had family members who stopped talking to me as they listened to what they were being told and went on to bad mouth me.

This was all because I stood up for myself, I went against the grain, and it was because my time off showed me how to love and respect myself. I learned how little I actually respected and loved myself before. I finally knew how I should be treated and I was not going to let anyone treat me any different, I was finally breaking the shackles.

Time can be a healer

Time can heal. Love comes in many different forms and when one of these is taken away from us we can feel incomplete, distraught, grief stricken and heart broken.

You might not even realise how much you love until you feel heartache, but remember that love you felt, it is not broken, it is still here, it has just been separated in physical form for a time. Energy never dies.

Make that choice not to get up in the morning feeling all doom and gloom.
Choose to remember that feeling of love.
Choose to take the time to heal.
Choose to leave yourself heal.
Choose to live.
Choose to be happy.
Choose to love.

Memories and laughter can be the one thing that we all really need at times.You have to remember as well that death is not the end for anyone, it is only another part of our journey. No matter what religion or ethnic background you come from, there is always a form of an afterlife.

Embrace Life

Be grateful for every morning that you have the opportunity to wake up.
Be grateful for every breath of air that you get to breathe.
Be grateful for all the different colours that you get to see.
Be grateful for all the smells that you love.
Be grateful for everything that you touch and hear.
Be grateful when you go to sleep at night.

Give thanks for the roof above your head, the bed you get to sleep in, the clothes you are wearing and the shoes upon your feet. Be grateful for the food and water that pass your lips. Do not take life for granted, you should appreciate everything that you have.

Life is as beautiful as anything you will ever get.
It is the most precious gift that
you can be given or you can give.

We, as humans need to never give up hope, we need to have the belief that everything will get better, it is this belief that strives us on, it is this belief that gives us hope, it is this belief that will help us get up in the morning and get through our darkest days.

Without hope, the world would be a very gloomy place, there would be nothing, it would be dense, it would be colourless.

It is the hope of business people that gives us shops and products, for without hope that no one would buy their products there would be no business, it is the hope of peace activists for peace, without that hope there would be more war.

Without hope, no one would ever even try to follow their dreams.

A LIFE THAT'S GOOD

We all think that we need this, we have to buy that, we have to look this way, we have to go here and that we need more than we have. It is nice to have nice things, to look good but it is not nice to have to behave a certain way to fit in.

Who decides WHAT is right to fit in?
Who decides WHO is right to fit in?

It is the people who are always striving to fit in that are the ones that are fighting their own demons, they are the insecure ones.

Do not judge them, we have all been them at some stage in our life, we have all tried to fit in, whether it be with the cool kids in school, the office crew, the other parents, even with our own family.

We are led to believe that we have to be a certain way, we are led to believe that we have to believe in certain things and if you have your own opinion or act differently, it threatens the peace of those around us, you make them question what they believe to be right, and this can stir up mixed emotions within them, they might strike out against you, they might even shun you and heaven knows they might even laugh at you.

But, do you know that you have the power inside of you, to care so much that you do not even care, to love so much that you do not let it affect you?

You have the power to be just you and that is all that matters, it is a life that is good, a life that is magnificent, just like you are.

Paint a little picture

Everyone has this perceived notion and idea of how every single person that we meet or that we know, should act and be.

That is not the case, with every person that you know or meet you will only ever know them from your own perception and how much that they want you to know about them.

We make our assumptions of other people as we see from our own perception, also from what they want and what they allow us to see.

Think about it, we only see from our perceptions and what people allow us to see.

We do not know what anyone is going through at any given moment in time, so be careful of the way you treat someone and talk to someone.

That stranger standing next to you in a queue wanting to talk might have no one at home to talk to.

The person working on the till offering no smile today could be just after finding out they have an illness.

The smile that you see walking towards you in the street could have a heart that feels completely broken.

How you talk to someone can be taken up completely differently to the way you intended it to be. Sometimes we say stuff unintentionally and end up offending someone. We have to be more cautious and sensitive with the words we choose to speak and especially with the tone of how we say it.

As the old saying goes
"If you have nothing good to say then do not say anything at all".

Letting the actions or the non-actions of others affect me

It is very easy for me to say do not leave the actions or in some cases the non-actions of others affect you, but in true life, it is very hard to separate from others and know how or when it is affecting you.

I once found myself awake at 4 am in the morning after struggling to fall asleep at 2am, there was no way that I could get back to sleep.

I lay down in the dark, too tired to move, I did not bother doing what I knew I needed to do, I did not talk to my guides, I did not meditate, I did not even bother to get up to get a drink, I just could not sleep and I did not even turn on the television or pick up a book to read to occupy my mind, I just lay there in the dark, questioning the actions of other people towards me. I was filled with dread and anxiety. I was hurt and felt betrayed. What I came across could have merely been a mistake but I started to question other people's motives, and let it take over my mind where it grew bigger and bigger.

Twenty-four hours later, after struggling to keep a migraine at bay, after struggling to keep my eyes open and struggling to keep my mood upbeat to enjoy the day with my son, I realised that what I would advise someone else to do is one of the hardest things I find to do myself sometimes, I gave my power away.

I love to get up and exercise first thing in the morning, I struggled to get out of bed and do any exercise for a few days. I tried to make myself presentable, that day I found it hard to be even present.

When I got out of bed, my hands were numb, my lips had pins and needles, my vision was blurred, my voice sounded different in my head, my eyes were sore, I could not concentrate.

How did I let this happen to me?
How did I let the actions or non-actions of others affect me so much that I was merely a shadow of who I am?
How did I give someone that much power over me?
How did I not realise that I am worth far more than that?
Why did I allow their actions or non-actions affect me so much that I doubted and questioned who I am?
Why did I let them have so much control over how I felt?

Simple answer is I gave away my power.

I did not respect or love myself enough.

I did not own my voice.

I did not honour who I am.

I gave other people the permission to treat me as they pleased.

When I realised this, I took back my power, I decided that my life is in my control, I am the car and I am the driver, and I choose which road I take. I have learned after those last few days, if I was respected, they would have trusted me. I had struggled and sweated for years for them and this was my thanks.

Now the dread is gone, I am a magnificent person who deserves a better life, a life that I am passionate about and I needed for that passion to return.

People are going to test you and not all people are going to respect you but do not let it stop you as this is their issue and not yours.

If this is the way that they are going to treat you, just sit back and imagine how they treat and feel about themselves.

Everyone is entitled to their own opinion and to choose what they want to feed their own minds and what they want to believe but do not let anyone disrespect your wishes and opinions, even more importantly do not disrespect theirs either.

Believe in yourself as much as you believe in every single other person.

Why place the blame?

Do not blame yourself for things that you may have done or think that you might do.

That is not who you are, the past must be left in the past whilst the future quite simply does not exist, the only time that you have is now, so do not worry about tomorrow.

Every morning that we get to wake up is the first day of the rest of our lives. Everyday that you get to look down at the ground rather than up at it, is a good day. There are plenty of people who wish they could have your life, no matter how bad you think it is at the moment or whatever it is you are personally going through, know that there are other people in this world who wish that they had the life that you are living.

Everything happens for a reason, breathe, sit back and relax, for there is no need to worry. Have trust and faith that everything will work out the way it is supposed to.

If at times, life throws you a handle, grab it, but know that if it doesn't, you will find your own way, knowing that you can and keep the faith that you will find the right path for you.

WHY THE BATTLE?

What is the point in fighting with yourself?

What is the point of fighting with other people?

Does it make you feel good?

What advantage is it to you?

The answer is there is absolutely no point, it won't make you feel good and it is no advantage to you what so ever.

If you are fighting with yourself over past mistakes, you are fighting a losing battle. Mistakes belong to the past, and that is where they should be left. You might look at them as mistakes now but maybe they were simply stepping stones sending you on a learning curve.

You are not your mistakes, you make them, everyone makes them, then we learn what we can from them and do our best going forward.

Be true to yourself here and now, do not fight with yourself over what you should do or should have done, just trust that when the time is right, you will know in your heart what you are supposed to do.

What you see in the mirror is not just you. You are more than the body you possess, you are more than your face, you are more than your eyes, you are more than your nose, you are more than your hairstyle.

What you are inside of you is what really matters, your spirit, your heart, that is who you truly are.

Take time to get to know the real you.
Get to know the person staring back at you every time you look in the mirror, not just your reflection.
Look into your eyes, see your soul and go deep within.

You are not going to see eye to eye with everybody else, nobody ever will. There is no point worrying about it, and there is no point continuing the fight. That does not mean you are going to be best friends, you might not even talk to each other ever again but this is not about them or anyone else, this is about what will serve you better.

So, forget about it, let it all go over your head and be the better person, do not bother holding any grudges or grievances towards them, just know that you do not have to worry about it, do not question why or what is the problem, or how to solve it, forget about it and let it go, move on with your life.

Stop expecting you from other people

Do not define yourself or expect from other people what you do for yourself or for them. Stop expecting You from other people. Have enough respect and love for yourself to appreciate that You are You and you should never be surprised or expect others to treat you the way that you would treat them.

Just because you would do something for someone, does not mean that another person should or will do the exact same for you - they are not you. They must do what they must do to suit them.

So, set a standard for yourself and do not lower it to suit anyone else. If someone disrespects you, have enough respect for yourself to walk away and to not let it affect you.

I know that this is easier said than it is done, but why should you let the expectations or actions of others affect you, what you do or how you feel? Everyone reacts differently in situations, just because I would react some way does not mean everyone else will react the same way.

Be you, stop expecting you from other people, stop letting other people expect themselves in you and stop expecting you in them.

SEE IT THROUGH SOMEONE ELSE'S EYES

What I see through my eyes is completely different to what you see through yours. Who is to say that I am right and who is to say that you are wrong.?

We will all see life through our own eyes, our own experiences and our own beliefs. We will all have our own individual perspectives on absolutely everything.

You might look at a flower and think that is the most beautiful thing in the world whereas I might look at a tree and think that is. None of us are wrong, we just appreciate different aspects of beauty and we all have different opinions.

I might see everything with colour, you might see it in black and white, what you see is different to what I see, but we are looking through our own eyes and have our own opinions on it. Respect what is different to yours.

Sometimes what we really need, is to see from a different perspective and look through someone else's eyes in order to see how well we are doing or when we need answers that we cannot find ourselves.

Pot/Kettle

When it comes to our own mental health, people are still too afraid to express how they feel. They are afraid that by associating themselves with an illness or a disease that it makes it them. In this instance you have to choose your words wisely.

You are not the illness.

You are not the depression.

You are not the anxiety.

You are not the anger.

These are feelings and emotions that you are experiencing which is totally normal. It is how you find a way to cope is what matters. Every emotion is energy in motion, ready to be cleared and moved. Reach out for help if you need it, eat the junk food if you have to, go for a walk, exercise, lie in bed, do what is best for you.

No one can tell you what is right for you. The best way to find out what is right for you is by listening to your body, trust me your body will not lie. Take all the time that you need to get back to yourself and do not beat yourself up over it.

Whatever it is that you are going through, listen and learn from it. See what the triggers are and learn your coping mechanisms.

I went through a phase one Christmas after being non stop on the go for the year, setting up a few different businesses, ironically it was a wellness centre and working on numerous different wellness projects, I just hit a wall after I was criticised. There was a jealousy came in around me, of people that wanted to be doing what I was doing and they could not get over how good I was at doing it.

My downfall was that I was looking after everyone else besides myself, and at the time I was getting nothing in return from all these people. I forgot that I had my own business to run, and it was falling by the way side, as well as having a full time job. I did not exercise, I took to bed and Netflix, I just had to hibernate and refill my own pot.

I was at everyone s'else beck and call, I was supporting everyone but none of these people were supporting me back, they weren''t referring anyone to me, coming to my classes, or even doing something as small as pressing a like button on my social media posts but yet I was doing that for everyone else, whereas I loved doing what I was doing, it was a learning curve for me as you have to get something in return, why do for others if you are getting nothing back?

It is only now that I was beginning to realise how good I was at it and getting to know what I can do better. I dug myself into a hole and was finding it very hard to climb out of it. I had to rest, build up my energy and get back when I knew the time was right. The ironic thing about it is, what I was building up was and still is all about wellness and the importance of looking after ourselves - emotionally, physically, mentally and spiritually. I was not doing any of this for myself, I was too busy looking after everyone else, whilst neglecting myself, and my normal slogan is "you cannot pour from an empty pot".

It is the one scenario that I am often hit with, except now I am getting much better at looking after myself, and letting everyone else to their own devices. I have learned not to take on work for others if I am getting nothing in return. I know that if I do, no matter how good I do the job, no matter how much I want to do it, if it is not my business it is not my business.

If I get nothing in return or if I offer advice without being asked, I will be whacked.

Self Care is the Priority

You cannot pour from an empty pot, you have to take care of yourself before you can care for another.

Look after yourself, take those five minutes of peace and just breathe.

You are your number one priority.
It is not selfish and do not ever feel that it is.

If you cannot love yourself first and foremost then you cannot love another with all your heart or expect another to love you.

For all the parents out there who say they have not got the time to go for a walk or to go to a class or do something for themselves, think of it this way -

If you do not look after yourself, who is going to look after your kids when you are gone?

Prioritise yourself

One of the first mistakes people make is that they think that they need someone else to make them happy. First and foremost you have to be happy in yourself, everything else will fall into place after that.

No one should ever settle for less than what their energy tells them is right for them. It is not being choosy, it is prioritising You, the most important person that will ever be in YOUR life.

Be content in you and enjoy everything that you have, making you your number one priority.

Never settle for a love that is not different from anything you have ever felt before.

That love is when your heart beats so fast anytime you think of that person or you hear from them, your breath changes, your heart skips a beat and you have that tingly, all knowing feeling in your chest, it just feels completely right. It is being nervous and excited but completely at ease and comfortable all at the one time. That is the love that you want and need in your life, it is the love that you deserve.

LOVE SO MUCH THAT YOU JUST DO NOT CARE

This is a quote that was said to me years ago, and one I often think about and question from time to time.

Love so much that you just do not care.
Is it telling me that it is selfish to not care or is it telling me to love myself so much I do not care about anyone, or is it telling me that it is selfish to not love yourself.

At different times, it is a one that I often refer to and have a different meaning each time.

What it actually means is to love yourself and everyone else so much, unconditionally, that no matter what is happening you just do not care, it is not your business.

You cannot help anyone else unless you help yourself first. Look at the analogy of the air mask on a plane, imagine telling a parent to put it on yourself first before they put it on their child, it seems so unrealistic, but you cannot help your child if you do not put it on yourself first.

OTHERS PEOPLE'S ISSUES AFFECTING YOUR MENTAL HEALTH

Other people's energies can play a huge factor in what you deem to be your own mental health.

Imagine that, sometimes we actually think that how we are feeling or the stuff going on in our heads is ours when it can actually belong to someone else.

If you are having any problems with someone or with a certain situation, take yourself out of the equation and hand it back to them.

Direct the energy back to them, imagine a mirror right in front of you so anything that they are directing towards you is going directly back to them. You can set the intention to have this mirror there at all times.

I had a situation for a few months where I would find myself for a few moments, at certain stages getting very angry, bitter, irritated and fighting with everyone, this is not my energy at all, whereas I know it is the energy of a person who has an issue with me.

But, did I cop it straight away - NO!
It took me a few hours before I even realised I was like that.

So for me, it was that person's problem so why should I carry how they feel with me? I shouldn't.
Why would I take on their issues? I shouldn't.

In hindsight this is very easy for me to say now, and it took me a few hours before I realised it but when you become aware, when you start to understand and know your own energy, you are able to determine what is yours and what is not.

Obviously it hit me like a tonne of bricks, to make me more aware of it and I had a lesson to learn.

Sometimes you need help as you cannot get all the answers on your own. What we can do for others is always harder to do for ourselves.

I am lucky that I have brilliant people who I surround myself with and we help each other, it was one of them that drew my attention to it.

Whereas now, first thing when I notice my self feeling like that, I know to send it back as it is not mine and I do not want it, but at times I do forget completely and struggle for a few days before I even cop on.

So how was this able to affect me - that person's thoughts were energy and there was so much malice behind it, it multiplied in frequency and hit me (the person who it was directed at). I was not fully in my body or grounded, not looking after myself like I should of been. I could of most likely mentioned them in conversation and wham I opened the doors.

So what did I learn from this?
If a conversation is not doing me good, shut it down.
If there is a way for me to hand over a situation, hand it over.
Have more respect and love for myself than any other person can possibly have.
Do not care what anyone else says or does, even if it is directed at me, it is not my problem to take on.

Check in on yourself every single day, see how you are feeling, check if it is yours and if it isn't, give it back.
See yourself letting them go, even just set the intention and let everything else flow.

You have enough to be carrying on your own, you do not need anymore hitchhikers or anybody else's crap.

DO NOT LIVE IN THE PAST OR IN THE FUTURE.

You can only do for you what you can do right NOW.
There is no other time other than NOW.

Worrying about something that has already happened is a waste of your time, you cannot change it but you can learn from it.

Worrying about the Future is a waste of your time as you do not know what is ever going to happen.

You can take all the tools and information from the past and use them NOW, to help you to create a future that you want whilst staying in the PRESENT.

Everything changes so quickly, have a quick look back to a few months (without living in the past)
and look how every single person's life changed over night.

Do not let your mind wander into the future thinking all the worst possible outcomes -

THE HOW'S

THE WHAT'S

THE WHY'S

THE WHEN'S

THE IF'S

This is not living, this is merely existing, whilst creating unwanted anxiety and fear.

Try to stay with what you are doing right NOW, in this PRESENT MOMENT.

Always remember that there is no other time but NOW.

You cannot always control what goes on around you, but you can choose to control what goes on inside you.

MEDITATE DO NOT ISOLATE

We spend so much of our time connected to our jobs, our phones, our social media accounts that we forget to connect to what truly matters, connecting with ourselves, connecting with the people who are there in our lives - our family and our friends.

Take the time to yourself to find the answers that you need but do not isolate from all the people around you. We can do a lot of things on our own, but we also need people around us to help us and keep us grounded.

We all tend to look for the answers on the outside rather than going within ourselves, asking our own internal computer system. If we feel down or we are feeling sick, we actually google what is wrong with us rather than questioning our bodies and searching for the answers that we seek within.

The majority of the time a cold will be diagnosed as a life threatening illness. If we are feeling down it could be from strolling through Instagram and Facebook, looking at other people's photos, letting us see into what the majority of them make up to be their lives.

Energy travels everywhere, it does not matter if it is in person or on the phone, we can still take on other people's energies.

We tend to forget what we are feeding our minds and putting into our energy systems on a daily basis, from the content that we are scrolling on social media, the books that you read, the music that you listen to, the conversations that you have. These all have a major impact on how you feel.

You can have everything in the world, all the riches you dreamed of but what is the point if you do not have anyone to share it with. We spend so much time worried about what everyone else has or thinks, that we never count our own blessings and appreciate what we have. There are plenty of people who would be happy and grateful to be in your shoes.

Our bodies hold the answer to every single question that we have and that we want to be answered but we have either forgotten or were never told how to listen or connect to ourselves.

Anything that you need to know you already do, you just have to re-learn how to disconnect from the world and reconnect to yourself, listening to and trusting to the voice within.

Feeling the emotions

You feel guilt, you feel pain, you feel anger, you feel regret but ultimately you also feel love. Love can and will conquer any feeling. Love is what we are here to do. A house is only bricks and mortar, but a house with love is a home.

We want peace, we want friendship, we want family but none of them are achievable without love. Look how good you feel when you love, it is like walking on air, you feel like dancing, you feel happy. Love is the only drug we need.

On the other hand, if you feel hate, it rips you up, tears you apart, causes worry, depression, anger, all of which is are being fed into your body so just imagine the consequences then if you let hate consume your mind - tiredness, sickness, burnout, etc.

Treat your emotions like waves, they will come and go. Feel every feeling, acknowledge every feeling but do not beat yourself up over them and do not dwell on them for too long.

At the end of the day, you are not what you are feeling, what you are feeling is an energy.

Love is the energy that you need to overcome everything, love is the energy that is the key to the kingdom.

Emotions are essentially energy in motion.
Emotions come in waves so allow them go back out with the tide. Most importantly do not feel guilty or hang on and dwell about them.

Do not be hard on yourself over anything that you are feeling or going through, there are plenty of people in your life that will be hard on you, so do not choose to be one of them by being hard on yourself. Every emotion and feeling that you will ever have is natural, you will always get negative feelings but the negativity is only based on how you view it and deal with it yourself.

Flip the switch on your perception.
Every emotion and every thought has a reason,
so if you are feeling uneasy about one of them,
sit with it and ask what is it trying to teach you.

Come to your own conclusion

When it comes to other people, do not take any notice of their opinions, come to your own conclusion. Other people will want you to have the same opinion as them, that is entirely to satisfy their own needs and not yours.

I come from having worked in a business for years that dealt with hundreds of people. If I listened to other people's opinions I would not like anyone. I always tend to look at people and think I do not know what is happening in their lives to make them the way that they are, so I pay no attention to what other people think of others.

At the end of the day, all we really have to do to be truly successful in life, is to be nice to people, to take no notice of what anyone else says and to come to our own conclusions, all the while realising that even though we have our own opinions, they do not really matter either.

I have seen marriages break down and people taking the sides of one partner and talking about the other.
None of us actually knows what goes on in anyone else's relationship.

None of us knows what goes on behind anyone else's closed doors.

None of us knows the conflicts or obstacles between two people.

We have to realise that it is none of our business anyway.

I have seen people take a dislike to someone just because another person does not like them. Half the time they do not even know why they do not like the person in the first place, so go with your own gut and trust yourself.

People get too caught up in situations that are not theirs to get caught up with in the first place.

Stay in your own lane, playing your own game.

Find a routine but do not get stuck in the habit

Do not get stuck doing the same thing every day. Find a routine but continually break the habit. When I say get into a routine, I mean get into a routine of going to the gym, going out for a walk, looking after yourself, a routine of self-care but ultimately do not do the same thing every day as you will get bored, and your energy will get stagnant. By constantly changing up what you do, it will keep your energy flowing and you won't get as bored.

I used to be a creature of habit and routine, everything organised down to a tee. Now I still do to a certain degree. I like to go to the gym for 7.30/8 am in the morning, it would be the same faces, but instead of breaking this routine, I change up what I am doing in order to stop me getting bored and it being like "ugh I must go to the gym".

So instead of walking the same route every day, go the opposite direction for a change. If you walk or run the same route all the time, you are only building up the same muscles and the other ones are not getting used at all, like your brain. Yes, your brain is a muscle in my opinion that constantly needs to be trained. If is seeing the same thing or even thinking the same thing every day, that is when the boredom kicks in. The brain needs to be stimulated.

It is like the "New Year New You Syndrome" where the majority of people will commit to going to the gym and getting fit, but 3 weeks later they pack it in.

Why?

Because they kept doing the same thing for 3 weeks in a row, the brain got bored, the body started getting used to it and they stopped seeing the improvement, they stopped doing it for themselves.

Find your own motivation and not anyone else's. It might be to lose weight, feel stronger, be healthier, look better. Whatever your motivation is, make sure that it is yours and that you are not just going with someone else's flow, it has to be yours for you to succeed.

Sucker Punch

You will get knocked, you will feel like you got kicked in the stomach and feel that nothing is ever working out for you. There are times that these things happen and it has got nothing at all to do with you.

You can have everything done right, perfected down to a tee, but it just is not meant to be, then other times if you do not stand in your own power, others will just come and knock you back.

You have to believe in yourself, you have got to believe that what does not kill you really only does make you stronger. You have to trust in yourself, in your vision, in your ideas and in your power. If someone knocks you, do not let it stop you from getting back up.

You alone have a vision of how your life should be or where you want it to go, no one else can see it or even understand it like you do, so do not let other people's visions or opinions of where you should be or what you should be doing, impair your vision.

Sometimes what didn't work out for you,

really did work out for you.

Challenge

You will always be given a challenge, no matter how good your life is going, no matter how much you want something, even if everything is going smoothly, you will always have some hurdles to overcome. You can be doing what you love, be with the one person you are destined to be with, there will always be times of stress and times of sorrow but ultimately there will also be times of joy and excitement.

You are not going to find all the answers at the top of the mountain. Everything takes work, and it is continuous, once you reach the top of one mountain, another one will appear.

No matter how far you have come, there will always be obstacles, that is life. How you decide to conquer all these obstacles will depend entirely on how you perceive them.

If you are going to face something with a pessimistic view, then there should be no shocks when you get hit ten times fold, whereas when you face it head on, full of optimism, then the battle is halved.

I went through a stage in a place that I worked in for a very long time, that I felt like I was being challenged left, right and centre, no matter what way I turned there was another challenge. This was a resolve in me that I had to beat, it was emotions within me that had to be healed. At the same time, it is not just about the emotions being stirred in me to be healed, it was about being a voice and not leaving other people being walked on, trampled on and spoken to horribly, or giving the power to someone else to think that they can go around treating people like this. It was about taking back my own power and giving back the power to other people who needed it, whilst also bringing someone back to our level.

Even though I am only responsible for me and what I leave affect me, by being responsible for me and taking action for me, I was also giving others the power to be responsible for themselves and take actions for how they feel and realise the way they are, if they choose to.

I could go around all day saying positive mantras, being unrealistic, only looking at the positive and end up getting no where, the same can be said for being negative (although I do prefer the positive as I would rather my brain and body hear that) but I have to acknowledge the yin yang effect also, we are going to be both negative and positive in different circumstances, with the negative you just have to ride the wave and work through the emotion, with the positive just enjoy it.

It was hard, every day was a struggle in there until one day it got enough for me and when I found myself being shouted at for no reason other than the "boss" being in a bad mood and as always, took it out on us.

The opportunity arose when they decided to pull the boss card and I quite simply, yet surprisingly very calmly turned around and said "maybe you should try to be a leader instead of a boss". Their face completely dropped in shock and off they scurried. I had spent a few years walking on eggshells, I was too afraid to stand up for myself or speak up as I knew the way I would be treated after. What ever came over me that day I just had enough. Anything that went wrong in the business, we were being blamed for.

A few months previous, I was verbally and aggressively attacked for being told something by another colleague. Ironically, the employee that told "the boss" dug themselves into a hole and was covering his own ass as he was the one that told the colleague that was telling me in the first place.

I spent sleepless nights dreading the next shift over the way I would be treated. I was being given jobs that the part timers should have being doing, being given jobs that had to get done ten minutes before my shift finished. I wrote a letter and carried it around with me stating my rights and noting the uncalled for abuse that I was subjected to. I never handed it over, but I realised that I was still carrying it with me and keeping that energy on me, I was physically carrying that energy through the letter with me daily.

I was a mere fragment of who I truly was. I knew I was being watched 24-7 by the boss and their blood hounds on cameras, if I sat down to take a break or if I was talking to someone for too long, they would appear out of nowhere. It was a power play to show me who paid the wages, it was a constant struggle to assert their dominance when there was no need to.

It is only now that I am looking back on it that I realised I was working for a bully and I had to learn to get my voice back, it was that day when I said "maybe you should try to be a leader instead of a boss" that the whole situation changed for me. They did not change in the slightest, but their attitude towards me changed as they realised that they would no longer get away with talking to me like that. It was this day that I began to not give a f**k.

Just a few simple words, said calmly and with confidence changed how I would face my day, it changed my attitude, it gave me the confidence not to be walked all over.

My spirit was not allowing me to be like that for anyone anymore.

You have to stand up for yourself no matter what the repercussions are, you have to forget about absolutely everybody else, no matter who they are, as your number one priority is you. If you are not being treated right, it will continue until you find your voice, until you respect yourself and know your value. If you do not own your value and worth, if you do not respect yourself, then no one else will either.

Stuck in a Rut

So, I found myself waking up, struggling to get out of bed, full of dread for the next few hours, wondering if they will be in good form, will I be listening to bitching, moaning, and endless conversations that I really could not care less about. I will be counting down the time until I sit into the car and start my journey home but wait a minute, this is not what life is supposed to be about. I should be doing a job that I love, that fills me with joy, that I jump out of bed in the morning and cannot wait to get there, the day flies by because I am having so much fun.

But how many other people felt like me?
I would say most of us at some point.
I knew that I couldn't just pack it up and put my faith that everything will work out, I have a child to look after, I have bills to pay like everyone else but I did not want to be doing or feeling like this.

I did not want to be stuck in this place and in this version of me, a version of me that I did not like, but what did I do about it?

The answer is I learned to just not care about anything or anyone else (to a certain degree) only me, I learned to love myself and respect myself so much that I found out what I love. I began to appreciate what I had and what this job was doing for me, ground myself and realised that if there is a problem, it is not always mine to solve or worry about, I only had to do what I was being paid to do.

The first thing I would do in the morning was to decide what way my day was going to go. I realised I have the power inside me to decide what I am going to allow to affect me.

When I did all this, I started to get excited about what my future is going to be. I started to visualise what I wanted my life to be, I set new goals and started to take the steps towards achieving them.

I had to change the way I looked at the situation in order to change how I feel. As soon as I started doing this, I started to change everything about being in that rut for me.
That feeling of being stuck in a rut started to slowly but surely become more moveable, and I began to realise that I was no longer stuck. We are only ever stuck when we allow ourselves to be.

THE FEAR OF THE FALL

Sometimes we set ourselves up for a fall.
We do not give ourselves enough credit for what we can do and we always think the worst possible outcome.

How about thinking the best possible outcome for a change?
Life can be so good, so why would we limit what we can have?

If we are going to think it's going to end up badly, surprise surprise that it does. All you have to do is pick yourself up, dust yourself off and try again but this time do it with the faith that you will get the best possible outcome. Change the way you think and change the way you feel.

Everyone thinks that in life you get the cards you are dealt but the reality is, you have the deck, you deal the cards and it does not matter how many you get, all that matters is what you do with them.

Next time something you do not want to happen happens to you, say "ah well that is that card let's choose another" and work on that. You have the power to change whatever you want, whenever you want.

We as humans need to never give up hope, we need to have the belief that everything will get better, it is this belief that strives us on, it is this belief that gives us hope, it is this belief that gives us life. Without hope the world would be a gloomy place, there would be nothing.

Fear is what cripples us, it stops us from dreaming, it stops us from living, so do not choose to live your life in fear. If you do not try something, you will never know if you can do it. Look at all that you could be missing out on by living your life in fear.

FIGHTING A LOSING BATTLE

You know when everything you do seems to go against you, when you just feel like crap, you just do not want to do something or go somewhere?

You just feel like you are fighting a losing battle.
Why not just accept it?
Realise that you might have lost the battle but the war you have been fighting every single day is still going on.

The war I refer to is your life, you have been fighting for things your whole life, you may not even realise it and we do not always win, that is life, we get knocked down but the greatest thing about us is that we have the ability to get right back up, we can choose to fight again.

Some things just are not meant for us, do not let that get you down. We can make a choice, we can either choose not to acknowledge what is happening to us or we can acknowledge it, accept it and look at it from a higher ground.

For example, just say that you went for a job that you really had your heart stuck on but you did not get it even though all the signals were telling you that you would. Look at the reasons that you probably did not get the job, say you wanted more time off to spend more time with your family, but the job involves working a lot of weekends and unsociable hours.

You want to leave your work situation but cannot seem to find any job, look at what is holding you back, what is the cause of you wanting to leave?

Is it the job itself, the people you work with, the environment, the atmosphere or is it your attitude and mindset that is preventing you?

Change your perspective on the situation, appreciate what you have and realise that ultimately if it does not suit you it is not going to end up in your lap. I guarantee you that once you change your attitude and mindset, new opportunities will open up.

Life is not about possessions, and it is certainly not about titles, so do not get stuck in that illusion.

FROM A SPARK TO A FIRE

What ignites your flame?

What excites you?

What motivates you?

What gives your life meaning?

What gets you to jump out of bed in the morning with a spring in your step?

That is actually what you are meant to be doing.

When you are doing what you are meant to be doing,

there will be no struggle and no obstacles that you will not be able to overcome.

You will have all the answers on how to do it without needing any help. Anything that is in the way will be cleared. It will come as second nature to you. You will not tire, you will not get bored and you will definitely not dream of something else.

What ignites you and excites you is what you are meant to do. This is what brings you to life, and it brings you to life for a reason.

A LITTLE CURSING CAN CLEAR THE AIR

I bet you did not know that one of the best ways to clear your energy is to curse. You know how good it feels when you say the F-word, how a bit of a rant can clear your energy completely, it can refresh your mind and make your body feel completely different when you are frustrated, irritated or angry, etc.

Cursing has the proven ability to help you clear your energy fast. These words have clear intent, they roll off your tongue for a reason and you can almost instantly feel the emotion as you say them.

When you verbalise something you are clearing it out of your system. You are letting it go and you are not holding on to it in your body.

The energy is being transformed into words and tones, the tone it takes will correspond with how you are feeling.

I had a client who could not curse, it went back to when she was a child and was told that it was wrong. She would come so far but kept getting caught up in the throat area, as if there was something stuck. Physically she could find herself grasping for air or feeling like she was going to vomit.

As soon as I made her aware that she had to curse to clear the energy, she really coiled into herself, as if she was a bold child. Her body language was as if she was after getting scolded for doing something completely wrong. As soon as she cursed, and after several failed attempts she eventually started to feel what she was saying, not just saying the word because I was telling her to, her energy completely transformed. She cleared the energy by cursing with the emotion and not feeling guilty for doing it.

Spreading your wings

When you are starting to spread your wings and leave the nest you will always have the people or situations trying to pull you back. This is nothing to do with how you feel, it is their own insecurities coming to the surface.

What you are bringing up in them is nothing to do with you, it is their insecurities of your situation.

Some people just do not like change but it is something we all have to go through. They will want to keep you the way you are and what you are doing, not for you but for themselves.

It is their version of you that they want to keep.

Do not ever be afraid to start a new adventure, especially if your nearest and dearest are not happy for you. They want to keep the version that they know of you in order to feel safe in themselves.

Change can be frightening for people, as it means they do not know where they stand with you, how your relationship with them will be, or even if you will have the same relationship.

The main thing is that you are true and honest to yourself, no one else really matters.

When you are living your life the way you want to, you will attract the right people and situations for you. When I started to mentally leave my job, as in the small talk and realising not to worry about situations that have nothing to do with me, that is not what I was there to do, there were little petty comments or expectations that I should come in when I was not scheduled to, and when I said no, like I would not of dreamed of doing before, there were expressions of shock and needless uncalled for petty comments.

Why would I or should I go in or be expected to, when I was not paid to and if it did not suit me?

People were trying to make me believe that I could not do what I wanted to by using little mind tricks whereas now I knew what they were up to, so I was able to just accept them for what they are, where they are stuck, what they are feeling and not let it affect me.

Sure, there were plenty of times that I did allow them get in my head, and I started to question myself, but I just had to keep bringing myself back to my heart and go with what is right for me.

People are going to have an opinion, no matter what you do, so why let it get into your head, in a nice way of putting it, just let them go (in a not so nice way of putting it - just let them F**k right off). You should never let it bother you.

You have an obligation to only you, to live your life the way you deserve to live it, not the way others want you to live it, you deserve to have the very best for you, not you living your very best life to suit other people's needs and wants of you.

Evaluate the people in your life,

if they are depleting your energy instead of adding to it,

then it is time to set them free.

You do not need anyone in your life

that is depleting your energy,

you need people in your life that bring you joy, love,

happiness and hope.

You know that feeling of just being totally free, not having anything stopping you or trying to get in your way, and even if they tried to there is not a hope that they could.
It is pure happiness, you feel the excitement burning inside of you, reaching to get out.

You can have that feeling any time you want.
Why not think of something you want right now?
It is not just a desire or dream, it is what you can have.
If you can picture it, there is a reason why you can.
It is within your reach and it is obtainable.

Spread your wings and get out of your comfort zone, it is time to branch out and have new experiences, living your life the way you want to live it. Do not believe that anything is impossible.

Impossible = I'm Possible

Not everyone has to know everything

Some details should be kept to ourselves. There is no need to be posting everything on social network sites, most people really do not care, and why would you pour your heart out to people that are just acquaintances? You are just filling them with idle gossip. Not everyone appreciates everything the same way as you do.

Everyone has this illusion that it matters how many friends you have on Facebook, how many followers that you have on Instagram, realistically it does not matter. Worse again people tend to think that these people have your best intentions at heart, the truth is they actually do not.

You are your own person, you have your own beliefs and opinions. What is the need to follow the crowd?
Why would you be bothered following the crowd?

Be confident in yourself and trust that you know what is best for you. Just because everyone else is doing this or has that or is going somewhere does not mean that you have to. Be you and do only what suits you.

THIS IS YOUR LIFE,

so why live YOUR LIFE to please other people?

THE BEST OF YOU

If people want the best for you, they set you free and are there for you when or if you need them, but they do not hold you back.

Keep an eye on the people who offer you support, they are the ones that you want in your life, not the people that crawl out from under the floorboards when they want a bit of you, when everything looks rosy.

Keep an eye on the people who wish the best for you and keep a check on the people who wish you ill. No matter what you do, you will have people that are striving for you to succeed and you will always have people rejoicing if you fail.

It is not always the people you expect that will wish you well and sometimes it is the people that you will least expect that will rejoice if you fail.

Always trust your inner voice and listen to your heart, it does not lie. If you know something is not sitting right with you, trust it, ask the following few questions;

Why is this not sitting right with me?

How am I feeling when I think of it?

What is the cause of this energy?

Who is the cause of this?

What is it trying to tell me?

It is getting your attention for a reason, so check out what the reason is.

The Shadow Effect

There is a shadow within us all and what we feed will ultimately succeed.

The Universe / God / Buddha / etc is not a being or an energy that is outside of us that we have to find, it already resides within us, and that is where we must search until we re-awaken.

What we must master is how to tap into that energy, inside of ourselves. All the "great achievers" knew that and that is how they have succeeded.

We spend so much of our time connecting or trying to connect with everything else, that we forget to connect to what truly matters, connecting with ourselves, connecting with the people who are there in the room with us - our family and our friends.

Hold up your hands, look at them and
I really mean look at them,
appreciate them.

Feel your heart beating
inside of your body.

Feel every breath that you take revitalising your body
and giving it life.

Now look inside your body,
close your eyes and take a journey throughout
your entire body.

There are a million little universes,
all operating together just so you can breathe,
just so you can feel,
just so you can exist,
just so you can be you.

That is God.
It is not outside of you,
it is within you.

Keep yourself rooted to the ground and soaring with the wind

You have to come to terms with who you are, even if it is just with yourself. Once you are honest with yourself, nothing can ever bring you down. You will be owning your own power, you will be owning who you are.

That does not mean that every Tom, Dick and Harry needs to know your business, heck no one actually has to know anything, what you do is entirely up to you, not anyone else.

Every single person's life is different, there are different factors that have to be considered for each individual person, everyone has their own story with a beginning, a middle and an end.

Each and every person is like a tree, with different branches coming out of it, these branches can relate to their different relationships to each person in their life. If someone cuts off a branch, it will affect the tree, but it does not mean that the tree is dead, it can grow around it.

Then you have the leaves, which represent something new every year, it is the opportunity to shed something old and grow something new.

We always have the choice to shed something old and grow something new. When you stop shedding, you are holding on, then you start to wither and die, you lose your beauty but you have the option to let go so you can thrive. You have to know when to let go, otherwise it will travel to your root and poison you from within, slowing infecting your body, mind and soul.

When you look at yourself as a tree, you are rooted into the ground, but you stand tall and strong, your arms are reaching out for everyone to see, but there are the hidden aspects to you, behind the bark that not everyone is concerned about, that tells a whole different story, one which the tree is happy in itself with but does not share. When you are cut you weep, you have the ability to heal yourself and your neighbour. Each year you shed what you do not need and regrow.

You even stand up against the strong winds that affect the environment around you, what you give out and the poison you take in helps every living being.

You do not leave the poison affect you,
you turn it into something positive and keep growing.

FEEL LIKE YOU ARE LOSING YOUR MIND?

Sometimes everything can just feel like it is getting on top of you, anything that someone says can literally annoy you so much to the point of breaking, you are biting your tongue so you do not let it rip and regret it. We can take on so much of other people's problems and emotions without even realising it.

Instead of just losing your temper, why not take two minutes to yourself, concentrate on your breathing, bring yourself back in to you. It is literally 120 seconds, there is no excuse not to.

Check if what you are feeling is yours or is it belonging to someone else. If it is belonging to someone else, just let it go. Visualise yourself letting it go, it is not your problem to deal with in the first place, you have enough to be doing in looking after yourself.

If it is your own, then do not beat yourself up over it, trust that it will be resolved, let it go.

Remember you do not live to work, you work to live.

This is a major problem with the majority of the people these days, they are too caught up in their work that they forget to make a life, neglecting themselves, their partners, their family and their friends, forgetting the whole point of work, forgetting that you work to live, you do not live to work.

You can have everything in the world, all the riches you dreamed of but what is the point if you do not have anyone to share it with?

What is the point of having lots of money in the bank but not making any memories?

What is the point of having the dream house with all the trimmings but you do not get to spend the time in it and you have to work all the hours you get just to pay it off?

We spend so much time worried about what everyone else has, that we never count our own blessings and appreciate what we actually do have. We forget that we do not need more and bigger to have a good life.

You may be very good at your job, but the day you leave or die, you will be replaced. Remember you are just a number at work, you are identified by your employee number, not by your outstanding contribution to the workplace.

Your workplace will replace you when you are gone but to your family you are irreplaceable.

One of the main things is that we all get caught up in is thinking that our work needs us, but we are all just a number, a number that can and will be replaced. We all need to work to pay the bills, to put food on the table and to send our kids to school, but do not bring work home with you. As soon as you walk out of the office, do not think about it, go home and spend time with your family, with yourself, go do something that you like to do.

WE NEED TO MAKE A LIVING BUT ULTIMATELY WE HAVE TO LIVE A LIFE.

It is easy for people to tell you to stick to your job, there is not much out there, it is hard to find a job these days or ask how will you pay your bills, how will you support your family? These are all very valid points, but that does not mean that it will not work out for you.

Why stay in a job just because it is convenient?
Why stay in a job that you hate?
Why stay in a job if every thought of it depresses you?

If you are feeling like this, then this is your message that there has to be a change.

Right do not just pack up and leave if you cannot afford to, but do start a plan, set the wheels in motion and keep your vision alive, save a bit of money to tide you over, know what you are going to do, and know it inside out like the back of your hand.

Take the steps that guarantee you to move but whilst doing so change how you feel about your current job or situation, appreciate it and find some form of happiness, that is when you will truly move on and flourish.

All you need to achieve anything in life is belief in yourself.

The possibilities are endless but you just have to believe in yourself and to not leave that belief falter.

You have got to have your own back,
you have got to look out for you,
you have got to be your own best friend,
you have got to believe in yourself more than you believe in anyone else.

Unexpected Routes

Know that whatever is going to happen is ultimately going to lead you to where you are supposed to be.

I know it is very easy to say not to worry.
If you lose your job and you have bills to pay, it is hard not to worry but maybe you need this time out to figure out what you need to do.

There are ways and means around everything, so listen to the voice inside you and trust what it is telling you to do.

Do not wallow in self-pity, jump out of bed in the morning and give thanks for having the time to do what it is that you want to do, retrain, take a course that you have always wanted to, just take this time to get your life in order.
Exercise and declutter, see how this will clear your mind, how it will make you feel good and happy with yourself.

Feel the love and feel the magic

Next time someone tells you that they love you, take notice of how that makes you feel. By feeling that love, you know you can give it too. You can have that feeling with you all the time.

Love is what we are meant to do, love can conquer everything, love is what we are here to do. Take notice of how good it makes you feel, and know that you can make another person feel like that.

Love might be a short word but it is the most powerful word that you can use.

You never know heartache unless you loved.
You would never feel pain unless you love.
You would never feel joy, happiness and peace unless you love.

Treat yourself better than they can

The way you treat yourself is the way you should expect others to treat you.

Why would you expect others to treat you any differently than the way that you treat yourself?

You have to set a standard for yourself and do not let that standard be low.

You know that saying about how like attracts like, well sit back and think about that saying. It is the law of attraction.

Why would you expect someone to treat you good if you do not treat yourself good?

The way you treat yourself and allow others to treat you
shows how much you are willing to tolerate
and the level of love that you have for yourself.
You are giving others permission to treat you
by the way you treat yourself.
You set the standard for what you accept.

Happiness and beauty do not start from the outside like the media will make you believe, it starts from the inside, it comes from the heart and feeling good about yourself. You can see all these celebrities on tv and magazines looking flawless, that is a false standard.

How many hours have they spent in makeup getting ready for that photo shoot?
How many hours has the photographer edited and photoshopped those photos so you would not even see one blemish?
How starving are some of these people just because they must walk down a red carpet to attend their movie premiere?
How many filters have they tried out before posting that selfie?
Have you ever wondered what they would look like without all that make up out on?

The pressure of being ridiculed and their bodies examined by everyone has them and us setting up an illusion of the perfect reality, which does not exist.

What is it all about?

Life is not about all the riches and titles that you acquire, it is about what you do when you see someone who needs your help, it is about offering a smile to a stranger who seems down, it is about being kind and never cruel, about accepting rather than judging, it is about being rather than wanting, loving rather than hating.

When you die no one is going to remember you for your titles or for your possessions, but they will remember you for how you treated them, how you made them feel, they will remember you for how you lived your life and the impact you made on theirs.

Life is about living.

WHY PUT A TAG ON IT?

Why label someone, just because they like or are into something different than you are?
People should not be treated like a clothes shop, and should not be labelled with a tag.

We are all different, that is why each and everyone one of us are unique.

Do not label someone just because their religion, their race, their sexuality or their beliefs are different to yours.

It is simple, they just like something different to what you like. It is easy to accept that not everyone likes the same food, or likes coffee or tea, so it should not be any different when it comes to life. It really is not a big deal, people like different things and there is no need to label them.
Everyone is equal, and should be treated as so.

Would you personally like to be walking around with a tag saying I am this, I do that, I like this?

People label for what they see as familiarity or they label for lack of understanding.

People judge because they think they have the right to.

In the world we live in, people are either idolised like gods or looked down on like peasants.

The truth is there is no difference between one person and another, we are all deserving, we are all priceless, we are all unique whether it be a CEO in a company or a homeless person on the street.

Always achieve to be remembered for how you made someone feel rather than to be remembered for your job or what you have. Never strive to fit in a world, in a mould or to be someone that you are not, this world is made up of all different individuals, be yourself, that is what makes this your world.

No matter what area of your life people are going try to label you, if it is work, parenting, friends, sexuality but do not label yourself and put yourself in a box to suit everyone else.

If you put yourself in a box, you are putting yourself in chains, and you are tied to that for the rest of your life, no matter how much you try to break free.

Ignorance is Bliss

I got into a conversation a few years back and it was an eye opener to me. When I say eye opener, I mean it showed me that I am thankful for what I am not and who I will never be, for the opportunities that I as a "white" guy have, for the injustices that I as a "white" guy growing up never had to face.

I am thankful for always having a roof over my head and never having to worry about where my next meal will come from.

I am thankful for my parents, who reared me to always stick to my own beliefs, listen to the opinion of others but to always have my own opinion. I am thankful that they showed me how to love and respect every single being, no matter what colour, race, religion or sexuality, that they may be. I am thankful that they have showed me the way to raise my son.

Apparently, I am a "do-gooder" and we are the problem with the world.
We are the people that tore down the borders and "let everyone in".
Borders are man-made, the world was not created with borders.
I would rather be a "do-gooder" than a "do-hater".

What actually amazed me was that in the 21st century, racism was and is still present in everyday life. Trump is not only in America, he is everywhere. He represents all that is wrong in the world and he showed his face to me in the form of 2 people who I have "known" for years and actually respected before, who I thought would be more open minded due to the fact that one of their grandchildren is of Asian descent and the other should know the injustices that people face due to their child having certain disabilities.

So apparently….
The only people who do U-turns in the middle of the street are black people...
They get absolutely everything for free...
They are all the same...
It is our taxes who are paying for them...
They do not work and oh yeah, they do not want to work.

This list could go on for quite a bit but seriously like "WHAT THE FUCK??", talk about pure and utter Bullshit...

I am not one who is easily offended, and normally do not pay any attention to closed minded individuals like this.

But what actually really offended me was the attempt to justify this way of thinking, even though I have black family members and friends.

I am under no illusion that I could change the way that they think. I would not even be bothered trying to. I respect that they have their opinion, and that is their right to have it, I just think that it is a pretty sad existence that you can have so much hatred for someone, who you do not even know, just because of the colour of their skin, the religion that they follow or the person that they share their bed with.

There are Irish people who do not work which is not due to their own fault and there are Irish people who simply do not want to work. I am pretty sure a few Irish people have done U-turns in the middle of the street. I am also pretty sure that if there is a free bank, no doubt some Irish people have found it as well.

They are all the same, really? You can brand a whole race of people the same just because maybe you had a run-in with possibly one person of that race or was it just the way you were raised back then and never came to your own conclusion.

This is the world that we live in when:

- The top singers are black (Beyoncé, Rihanna,).
- The top actors are black (Denzel Washington, Halle Berry, Morgan Freeman, Viola Davis).
- The top sportspeople are black (Tiger Woods, Serena Williams).
- The most influential person in the world is black (Oprah Winfrey).
- The second last president of the "United States" is black.
- We had Nelson Mandela, Maya Angelou, Martin Luther King.

People label for what they themselves see as familiar due to lack of understanding and lack of empathy.
People judge because they think they have the right to.
People judge because they are afraid.

In the world we live in, people are either idolised like Gods or looked down on like peasants.

The truth is there is no difference between one person and another, we are all deserving, we are all priceless, we are all unique.

It does not matter what colour your skin is, what religion you follow or who you love. We may all look different on the outside, but cut us open and we are all the same, we will all bleed.

Always strive to be remembered for how you made someone feel rather than be remembered for your job, your titles or your possessions.

Never strive to fit in a world, in a mould or be someone that you are not, this world is made up of all different individuals, be yourself, that is what makes this your world.

We all have different beliefs, we all prefer different things. You might not like what someone else believes in, likes or looks like but that does not mean you can disrespect them. You are not the Judge or the Jury, and it is not your right to put anyone on trial.

Treat others as you would like yourself, your parents, your children, your grandparents, your family and your friends to be treated.

Everyone is someone's child, no matter what age they are.

That person walking down the street, you do not know the struggles that they face every day.

THE "DO-NOTS" FOR A PEACEFUL LIVE

Do not take on other people's opinions, have your own, respect that others have the right to theirs but that does not mean you have to take them on.

Do not judge someone by someone else's opinion.

Do not expect others to do what you would do for them.

Do not expect the same level of respect you give to be given back.

Do not expect their values to be the same as yours.

Do not have any expectations of others.

Do not limit yourself.

Do not assume that you know everything.

Do not be closed to other's opinions but do not betray your own.

This is not religion, this is life. This is not a race, it is not even a war, unless you choose it to be and allow yourself to participate. All this is for your body, mind and soul to be at balance so you can live a more fulfilled life.

Wherever you will go

Know that you are not alone, it took the love of thousands to make you so those thousands are not going to let anything break you.

You have an army of angels, guides and ancestors with you at all times, ask for their assistance and guidance.

Quieten your mind, go into your heart and that is where you will hear them speak. They want the best for you, they know what is right for you so they will not put you wrong.

Close your eyes, take notice of how you feel, ask the questions, trust what you hear and how you feel.

Look Beyond

You only see the face, not the heart that lies within, or the struggles that anyone faces, all the hardships, or the embraces.

We really do not know anyone, what is happening in their lives, the trials and tribulations that they face.

The road we take can veer left or right, circle right around, come to a halt or go full throttle, that is the life we live, but what is for us will not pass us. Life is too short to get stuck in neutral or reverse.

It can be over in the blink of an eye, done and dusted, so choose not to worry about things that you cannot control or that has nothing to do with you, enjoy what you have now, in this very moment.

All you have to do is keep taking one step forward, it doesn't matter how fast or slow you go, once you keep putting one foot in front of the other.

The Future You

Are you having doubts?

Are you worried that your needs will not be met?

Are you worried that you will not exceed your expectations?

What are you fearful of?

You don't know what to do with yourself?

Not really sure where you are going?

You do not quite know what the next steps you should take?

Are you worried about what other people will say?

Why not try this, sit with yourself and ask your future self what you should do?

Your future self will not let you have any regrets.

Your future self has only your best interests at heart.

Your future self has all the answers that you need.

Your future self will help you succeed.

Your future self will not let you down.

When you start working with this version of you, there will be no obstacles, life will be so much easier and enjoyable.

No matter what you are going though in your life,

whilst always living in the now,

always ask ;

WHAT WOULD MY FUTURE SELF SAY?

HOW WOULD MY FUTURE SELF FEEL?

WHAT WOULD MY FUTURE SELF THINK?

HOW WOULD MY FUTURE SELF REACT?

WHAT WOULD MY FUTURE SELF DO?

Energy Speaks Tales from Beyond

THERE IS NO NEED TO FLUFF THINGS UP

I have a great belief that the energy that I channel is accessible to everyone, it does not mean that the person who walked barefoot up the stony mountain path with cuts and bruises all over his feet is going to be able to tap into the energy more than a mother breastfeeding her kid at home and screaming at the other two kids to pick up their toys.

I am not discrediting all the courses, heck I have done nearly all of them and there was a time that the people running them knew to automatically save my place before even asking me. We need to do courses in order to help us forget what we have been taught, but we have to trust ourselves first and foremost when doing energy work.

My main and absolute recommendations are you have to find and learn from the people who teach you to trust yourself more than anything. They teach you to listen to your own voice without a shred of doubt, they teach you to trust yourself and they set you free knowing that when or if you ever need them that they are there. They teach you to question everything, even them.

Courses have benefitted me amazingly because I got to meet like-minded people, the tutors that I retrained with were normal everyday people who had a no nonsense approach to this and you would be splitting your sides laughing coming out of it. That was the addiction to me, the laughter and the fun, it was what was missing from me for a very long time.

However, I do have a bit of an issue with words and labels though.

Lightworker, Healer, Fortune Teller, Faith Healer, Enlightened, the list could go on.

Nobody heals you but yourself, if a person calls themselves a healer, it is their ego talking. They are bigging themselves up. I have learned to avoid people that call themselves a healer at all costs.

In truth we can all do this if we choose to. I am not a healer, I do not heal your body, your body heals your body, what I do is I channel energy, I read energy, I work with energy. I can help clear your energy in order for you to heal yourself, but I do not heal you, you heal yourself.

I got a letter once from a well-known counsellor in the area where I live, saying how he heard about me and that he had a lady who was suffering, that maybe I could be of help to her. In the letter he called me a faith healer. It made my stomach turn. Whilst he would be coming from a very religious point of view, I think he misinterpreted what it is that I do.

I do not associate myself with any religion, not even spiritualist, because from my understanding and experience when you label something, the rules, regulations and propaganda comes into effect. People start putting themselves high up on a pedestal and diminishing others. So, I wrote a letter back to him explaining what it is that I do, to the best of my knowledge at the time, to which I never got a reply afterwards. I cannot really say that I was shocked.

People put labels on everything because they want to know all the ingredients and make it seem more difficult.

When everything seems more difficult, it makes them seem elite. These labels are actually doing more damage than good. People have a conception of how things should be, that everything is shiny and white. This is not the way it is.

Attending proper sessions with the right people ignite a flame in you to heal yourself and to learn. When this healing starts taking place, it is like a can of worms being open, more issues start coming to the surface to be tackled. Over the way things are labeled and explained, people think that one session should do all the work. That is definitely not true.

I am only highlighting these people as I see a lot of frauds in the business, people that are in it for the money and try to make it harder for everyone else. These people give the good honest people who have done the work a bad name. The people that are genuine and are doing it from their hearts.

We see all these pictures of Buddha's, Gurus, Yogis and "normal" people meditating. They are portrayed this way to make you buy into a different way of life. The more outrageous, non conformative and least approachable something seems, tends to get people to spend more money and buy into that way of life.

You know that is not the way the real life is. We do not have to dress like a Buddha to meditate, we do not have to dress like a doctor to help people, we do not have to sit in that awkward position to meditate, we do not have to be able to do a headstand.

This is all the illusion that the media and some practices are making us believe. All you have to do is be you. It is your energy that attracts people, that help people. It is not you dressed up as someone that you are not.

You are the magic so there is no need to create an illusion around it.

When energy takes over, when you trust in what you do, when you trust in the energy that is guiding you, when you trust in yourself, without a shred of doubt, it will take you to a whole new level.

When you find people that you can learn from and that want to bring out not only the best in you but the best in them also, it makes the process a whole lot easier and lots more fun. As they say, there are different strokes for different folks so everyone has to find what suits them.

We are all unique individuals, what I do is what comes from inside me, the magic comes from within not from the outside. The right person to help you is the person that ignites your flame to keep shining.

I will try anything, once it's not bullshit, strapped together with a load of rules, regulations and way too airy fairy.

I can answer so many questions but for every answer I can give, I have a question too.

Let go of everything you thought that your life would be and embrace everything that your life actually is.

The following stories are just some of my own experiences just to show what it is I do, to explain a bit more about energy related work and for me to eventually put it on paper so I know as well.

Fairy Good Time

I was running my first weekend retreat in the home of an amazing lady called Mary Madison. Actually, this was my first time doing any kind of group work. The energy for the weekend was absolutely beautiful, the people that attended were smashing, and the weekend went swimmingly well. It was all fairy energy which is powerful, joyful, fun and mischievous. I remember leading one meditation and everyone just completely conked out. I could feel all the energy coming in from the land and the sea. It was then I realised how powerful the energy was and how lucky I was to be holding this space.

On the Sunday evening when I finished up, I packed all my items away into my bags and double checked, even triple checked that I had everything. When I got home I could not find my iPad, and it is the one thing that is stuck to me like glue. I can specifically remember packing it into the bag, along with the speaker I was using.

I knew and I could remember putting it into my bag. Eventually I rang Mary to settle my mind and make sure that the iPad was there. Mary went out and checked, then she rang me back to tell me that there was no sign of it. Something in my head was telling me that I would have it back in 3 week's time when the fairies were ready to go home.

Exactly 3 weeks later I got a phone call from Mary, she said that when she walked out into the cabin that evening, right there in front of her eyes was the iPad, in the exact same spot that I was using for the weekend. She said how herself and another girl looked through the whole place the last few weeks and it was not there.

The cabin was used by lots of different groups in the few weeks, there would be storytelling groups, retreats and people that visit Mary for a reading use the toilet inside there, not one person in those three weeks saw the iPad.

The story actually goes that where I live is a fairy kingdom, and there was a wedding taking place here. Some of the fairies from Mary's land wanted to come up to the wedding so I was used for the spin and when they wanted to go back home the iPad reappeared, thus them hitchhiking a spin back down with me.

Psychic Surgery

I was taking part in a group training session and one of the skills that we were learning was how to perform a psychic surgery. Remember that this is as energy work so just to be clear there are no surgical tools required, no knives just energy leading it.

There was a lad lying down on the plinth and a woman working on him. As the surgery was being performed, she was working more over his groin area. Now just to be clear there was no physical contact what so ever, the lad did not even know where her hands were, but when he woke up, the instructor asked him how he was feeling and how he found it, to which he replied, "I felt like I was being pulled".

Well that was myself and the person who was sitting next to me totally gone. There were tears coming down our faces, we could not be consoled. This was one of the major importance's of having a down to earth instructor. Whereas if we had another instructor, he would have kicked us out for laughing but how could we not laugh, so instead he took a break for a few minutes and we still went back in as giddy as two little school kids.

BUTTERFLIES

I was running an online charity fundraiser for a cancer service for a very close friend. My energy was absolutely buzzing through out the whole month it was taking place. I had ideas bursting out of the seams. It was during Covid so everything was donation based and online as we couldn't hold any other fundraising events. I was writing articles and posts on topics that I would not have a clue about. In all the online posts I always included pictures of butterflies.

My friend wanted to pay me for all the work that was done but there was no way I was taking any money from her, as this was a very close charity to her heart. It eventually dawned on me to ask her what is the story with her and the butterflies. She told me how the butterfly always represented her sister who died and was one of the main reasons she was running the fundraiser for this cause. It all made sense to me then. I was able to do all I was doing as it was not me that was doing it, it was her sister.

One of the amazing things about it is that two weeks after the fundraiser ended, I won the exact same amount of money that we raised online, in a local lottery draw.

The Rockstar

We had a family pet for close to 14 years. He was the baby of the house, we all adored him. He would travel everywhere in the car with my father, and would be out waiting for him to come home from work every evening. If you said the word "walk" he would be out jumping up and down at the cupboard where the lead was kept. If you said the word "bath", you wouldn't find him, he would be hiding in a cupboard with the door barely open. He would often take refuge in a cupboard when a person he didn't like would come to the house so they couldn't find him.

When my child was born there was a hint of jealousy from him, he did not really take to him at the time, especially when he realised that this child did not leave at the end of the day.

When my young fella was 4 months old, Rocky's health took a turn for the worst, he suffered a stroke during the night and you could see he aged almost instantly overnight. He lasted for a few weeks, with a bit of brandy every day to keep his heart ticking over but on the day that he died I got the phone call to come home from work that he wasn't right. I ran out of work without saying anything, got home and he was lying on the ground barely breathing.

With his last bit of energy, he got up and walked over to the chair that my child was in, licked his face, came back over to where he spent his first night with all the people that he loved around him, then when we were petting him he passed over. We were all heartbroken, but to see that he used his last bit of energy to give my child a kiss, showed that he was happy to go and was passing on his throne in this home to my son. It was like he was giving his seal of approval.

That night and the following few nights I woke up numerous of times. I could physically see and feel him lying right next to me in the bed.

Jealousy rears it's head

No matter what you are doing, if you are doing it well in the eyes of others, there will always be an element of jealousy and envy somewhere along the way.

There was one person who I trained with, never wished me good luck or congratulated me when I was part of setting up a business until they saw the way I sold out an event, then they were all about me, wanting a piece of me, knowing that I could make them money.

When I ended up going against my heart and organising the event for this person, my body went into total shock, headaches, pains in my stomach, low confidence, self-doubt and lack of energy were just some of the symptoms I began experiencing. I was being told not to do it, my body was giving me the answers. I had to seek advice on what was happening to me. I was told not to do it but they were given the dates and I felt that I could not go back on it as I would let everybody down, besides I also had major respect for this person.

I decided it was time to come out of the space suit and go into the business suit. I did learn that this does not work for me, I always lead with my heart, not the mind, so the faster I get it done, the better for me as I can step away from it, but energy is energy and it does not work like that. If you are not meant to be doing something, you will know that you aren't meant to do it, the signs will show up.

In the end, after selling out the event, I knew something was up as I got a text less than sixteen hours before the first appointment was to take place, enquiring about hotels in the area and transport, the things you should have booked with weeks, then literally eleven hours before the doors opened I got a text that they had to cancel last minute, but instead of panicking, I never felt such relief. What did annoy me was the fact that the decency was never shown to me with a phone call or an apology. A few days passed before contact was made and by then I was done.

I did not even realise on how much of a scale it was affecting me, it was like a million knots in my stomach were suddenly untied. It affected me from day one, I kept putting off organising it until I had to, and anyone that knows me knows that if I am organising something, I organise it well. I knew it did not feel right to me from day one, but I went ahead and organised it anyway, choosing to go with my head instead of listening to my heart. I felt like I had no choice but to organise it. I filled up every appointment in less than two hours of announcing it, but I was affected right up until it was cancelled.

Looking back on it now, I know I was being protected, I was not meant to do it, that person was not meant to be there from day one, the energy was protecting me by stopping them coming and showing me that I had to break free. The unusual behaviour that they showed from day one with not wishing me well or congratulating me was not the usual behaviour from them. It was showing me that I did not need them anymore. I needed to break free and find my own path, which I never would have done had they not been given the dates and cancelling.

Due to the huge respect and admiration I had for them, I would not have realised how much their energy affected mine until I started organising the event. I hold this person in high regard but I would not have found or trusted in myself if I was still clinging to them.

Stranger Things

I attended a weekend course in the United Kingdom, and on the Saturday night there was a seance with, in their eyes, one of the best and most renowned psychic mediums of our time.

We were all gathered in this big old library, the lights were turned off, they asked everyone to hold hands and sing to raise the vibration. Anyone that knows me knows I absolutely detest this type of thing, I cringe. I never needed to do anything like this to connect and it always feels too movie like and airy fairy for me.

So, I am sitting there in the room, my eyes are rolling about, I do not want to be holding hands with anyone. I am the type of person that is brutal if someone even tries to hug me. I like my own personal space, as well as thinking about the sweaty hands, I am thinking of the germs, did the person on my left wash their hands after the toilet (note this was years before COVID).

So, the lights are off, they are all singing, except for me because I am thinking how can I wipe away the tears from laughter and cringing from my face when these people at either side of me are holding my hands, the medium is sitting in his box, (presumably asleep as it takes him so long to say anything - 30 minutes to be precise).

In the whole two hours he had three messages, two for people in the group and one for a fellow lecturer sitting with him. In my eyes if you are supposed to be one of the top psychic mediums in the world, and you have a room full of people, you will have a lot more than 3 messages.

There was supposed to be a spirit of a boy talking and running around the room. I felt him myself at one stage by my legs but his voice was coming from all around the room. I forgot to mention also that there was no access to this room at any other time throughout the weekend. So, my logical thinking on this, is that there are speakers put up in the room, when the room is in total darkness. I mean it was so black inside in the room that your eyes could not adjust to seeing anything. They had someone going around the room throwing toys about and brushing off people.

People want the wow factor, but to me this place had lost the belief in themselves and couldn't deliver the content that should have been delivered. I believe in raising the vibration, but spirit will come with just music playing, with good intention or when there is a big crowd gathered in a room and a good channel. It is like a radio station, if the reception is bad, the content will be the same. Either way if it was not set up, I would find it hard to believe that only three messages were delivered.

Annoying Angel

One of the first courses that I attended was with a woman who really talked herself up. I thought from the way she advertised that she seemed really good, approachable and positive but boy was I in for a shock. She was actually a nice enough lady, and from what was written on paper she seemed like a good fit to learn from, as this was my first time taking steps to learn something new, this was a safe reliable step.

There were not many options for courses like there are now and that is not even that long ago. It was for three full days and I paid in advance so I had to make every day. Then it ended up it was just me and her for the three days. There is definitely safety in numbers and it makes the process on every one so much easier.

For the whole three days, all I listened to was her family problems, how her website had been hacked and all that I am doing wrong (in her eyes). I was totally drained from the experience. If she was not talking about her family issues or criticizing me, everything I was learning was being fluffed up and made look way too more complicated than it actually is.

This was all at the start of me coming back to myself and even though I was drained by her, she was one of the only people offering courses at the time, so I was addicted to anything of this nature but I always had something telling me in my head, go do it but stick to your own devices.

To prove how much I wanted to learn I enrolled in another course she was doing, luckily it was a one day only course. We were in the room and everyone starting chanting, my only luck was that I was in the corner of the room out of nearly all view of everyone else, because I am sitting here, tears coming down my face, thinking why do they think you have to do this and hoping that the day would end soon.

Looking back on it now, this was all my guides way of getting me to know them, they were putting me into situations, places and doing things that I know do not have to be done that way. They were leading me on my path to finding the right people to learn from and showing me the people who not to learn from, and most importantly teaching me to have faith, to listen and to trust in myself, learn to listen to the voice within.

Reflexology Nightmare

I won a reflexology treatment with a woman who does nothing but portray herself as a healer and rants on about her healing abilities. I would be cringing now when I see this woman's posts on Facebook, it came to the stage that I had to block her profile.

Of course, I did not realise that until after I had the treatment but sure we all love a good nose, it was free and there was nothing to lose. It was my first time going for reflexology, and to be honest I am not too pushed for another session ever.

This is what can happen when you do not choose your therapist, and your therapist chooses you, you can get a complete turnoff.

I was greeted at the door by a big warm smile, that was grand. She explained the treatment, that was grand too.

BUT the very next minute she started telling me how she is a healer, that she has this natural healing ability and all the ailments that she cures. I just wanted to get out of there as fast as lightning after hearing all of this. She is telling me to pick an angel card and we will do a reading, so I obliged and picked out a card but for her to look the card up in the book and read it aloud to me.

In my opinion someone picks a card, you read the card/ the energy/ the relevance, not the book, especially if you are drawing a card for another person.
So how do you read the card? You look at the message, you look at the colours, you look at the picture, you tap into your client's energy, and why this card was handpicked for them on this day whilst always being in your own energy, then you read. You check what you are feeling and holding whilst holding the card. You check what comes into your mind.

The first thing I said to her when we went in to her treatment room was "what is the story with the chair and your father?" Her face just dropped, and asked how did I know that he gave her the chair.

I remember lying on the table, the sun was shining brightly and all I was wishing was "will this please end so I can get home and relax in the sunshine". I was just constantly listening to how she is a healer, her ego was crazy and to be honest, I came out of there feeling a lot worse than when I went in.

August Rush

I always emphasis about minding your own energy and to know your own energy, but sometimes this is not possible all the time. I was on bed rest one week, my system was totally wiped, so when I am not strong in my physical energy, this seeps through to the rest of my energy systems (mental, emotional, spiritual) and if I am not careful I can take on anything.

When I was recovering from the illness, I was cutting the grass and I thought of a friend thinking I must ring her, how I had not talked to her in ages, next minute my back gave way, I could hardly walk. I just thought I must have twinged it moving about.

I had to call down to my uncle's house later that evening, so I asked him about my back, straight away he detected what was wrong and said that I let her energy in around me, she was going through something and wanted to talk to me about it. As soon as he said it, I was back walking normal and the pain went in my back.

Yet an hour later, same thing happened me, my back was gone again. I contacted my uncle again and he told me how I had not cleared the energy completely and that it was still lingering there, so I was able to get rid of it now.

I was grand for the next few hours until bed time and there goes my back again. It was too late to contact my uncle and I did not want to look like a pain in the butt about it either, even though this time I knew it was something different. We were going on a day trip to Tralee the following day and I said it will be grand in the morning. My back got worse during the night, but we still went for the trip in the morning. I was in no pain when I was sitting down only when I stood up or walked, I actually needed a stick to keep the pressure off me.

Another person would have cancelled the trip but I knew my young fella was looking forward to the swimming and mini golf. I didn't want to let him down so I suffered on in agony. I did not want to pester my uncle for the 3rd or 4th time about it so I text another person who straight away told me how I took on the energy of a family member, as soon as he said it, I was back to normal again. Pain free and able to run around the mini golf, even do a bit of shopping. It came again, rang him again and cleared it up again.

It didn't last for long though, as on my way home, you will have guessed it by this stage so I won't repeat myself and sound like a parrot. Even though there would be no issue contacting my uncle and the other man, I knew this was for me to do this time and I was also slightly embarrassed that I could not contain or control my energy and kept letting other energies in around me.

So, when I got home, I sat outside on the porch of the playhouse, lit sage pressed play on my iPhone, closed my eyes and started breathing. I detected a number of energies in my system.

I was transported to a mountain, one we drove past on the way home, but I was there from centuries before now, it involved a family of husband, wife and son. The August Rush music was playing in my head all the way home, so this was giving me a picture of who I had to help.

The main bit of the situation that I remember is that the boy was a lost spirit, who died on the mountain, and was looking for his parents, who were also lost and looking for him, all separated in their own grief that they could not move on after they had all died. This is where August Rush came in to give me the picture. I was able to guide him to his parents, where they were all able to eventually reunite. I remember the feeling that came over me watching them all reunited, I had tears of joy and felt the warmest glow over me that I never ever felt before.

Another energy on that day that I took on, was the spirit of a deceased cyclist who was knocked down on the road a few months previous. Part of his spirit was still stuck in this world and he had not fully moved over. This can happen for many reasons, especially in times of accidents or if they are leaving family members behind.

The importance of this day showed me how if I do not look after myself, I will be hit with everything in the kitchen even the sink. I was meant to pick up all these energies not just for me to learn but to help all these people find peace.

People will be thinking that "oh my god these people haven't moved on and is this is what really happens is when we die". From my understanding, these were fragments of the people's energy that were left behind and they are calling them home, that is where I came in to help.

I over medicated instead of leaving my body fight the illness itself, over medicated instead of over meditated. I kept downing tablets which were affecting my aura and energy. Picture yourself with a big balloon around you, now when you are in your own body and energy, that balloon is full and there are no holes, but when your system is down there are loads of tiny holes in that balloon which is deflated but still around your body, so other energies can get into those holes then start half filling them up, taking over your balloon.

It is very hard to explain this to anyone, I can only tell my own stories and what it is that I have seen or done. I certainly do not have the answers to everything, I can only work with what I am given, it took me a long time to come to this conclusion. At the start I wanted to know everything, when I eventually gave up that thinking and appreciated what I do, I understand it better.

Blown away chest

I was running one evening in the forest that I normally go to, but half-way round I could not breath, it was like I was a 60 a day smoker.

Physically I was in brilliant shape, and I was well used to this run but I had to stop running, then I copped on that I was talking to myself saying this is not my chest, this is not me, then all of a sudden, I was chatting to an old woman who had a message she wanted delivered to her grandson.

I actually drove past her grandson on the way to the forest. The key to this was, I realised that it was not my energy, it was not my chest. I was in my own energy and was able to determine the message almost instantly.

What made this easier was the fact that I knew her grandson was open to what I do and would often chat to me about it so I was able to pass on the message without having to worry. What made the message easier was the fact that what I had to tell him was to make contact with a person whose card he actually put away earlier in the day. The grandmother was making sure that he did not forget as it was what he needed.

Last Rites

One Saturday morning when I was at work, I was cooking in the kitchen, next minute I knew I was chatting away to something or somebody, and it was telling me to send them for the last rites. I remember I was arguing with them that I cannot do that.

I didn't really think about it too much, as I thought it was a conversation I was having with myself, knowing that it was true, I pushed it to the back of my mind and didn't question it anymore.

Next day I got a phone call telling me that the person had died. I was wrecked with guilt of why didn't I tell them but it wasn't my place to tell them and if I did they could have ended up in a worse situation because of my intervention.

I was being trusted with the information as proof to me of what I do, to help me to have more confidence and trust in myself.

The message was very clear, even though it was on about a person dying and telling me to give a message, the message at the end of the day was for me, there was nothing that anyone could have done as the man's time was up.

There are times when you can pass on the information and there are times that you can't. You have to trust yourself and not feel guilty for your actions. Not everyone is open to hear, you have to be very careful what you say or don't say as you are dealing with people's emotions.

If I had passed on the message to them, I could have created a panic situation, I could have taken any bit of hope that they had, and I could have ruined their last few moments together. Alternatively, I could have given them the last few hours together, knowing that this was their last but would they have looked at the person who is dying, in love or would they have looked at him in pity?

Did the person who was dying want them to remember him as they do now or when he was taking his final last breaths?
I had a personal relationship to this family, so for me I had to choose that this man and all that came from beyond for him to pass on the message was for me, and it was for me to decide what was best to do with this message.

Connection to a Girl

Did you ever just meet someone and you had an instant connection? Not sexual or physical it feels like something more than that and you just cannot quite grasp what it is.

I was on a weekend course and the first person I came into contact with was a Danish girl. We saw each other outside and she reminded me of myself. She was strolling around, sticking to herself, we smiled and nodded at each other.

Over the course of the next few days this kept happening to us, we never ended up in the same group until the last day. At night time in the bar we were in separate groups but kept glancing at each other. There was a familiarity and a curiosity surrounding us.

So, this is what I mean about the connection. Here we are sitting in a mediumship demonstration. I am at the back of the room and she is at the front. The tutor is calling people up to give messages. My whole body language is saying no way but my knee is tapping like crazy telling me go. There was an excitement in my heart but a panic in my head.

I hate speaking in big groups and then she signaled me out to come up. Reluctantly my head is saying no but my body is saying go go go. It felt like something had taken over my body and it felt so good, it felt natural, I felt alive, I felt like I was home.

So here I am, standing on a stage in front of about 40 people, nervous and trembling, then all of a sudden, I start talking. I am still nervous in my head as I am not quite sure what is happening or what I am about to say.

Long story made short without going into too much detail, this girl's grandmother had come to me, as soon as I got up on the stage, I was staring at her because I knew it was for her. Everyone else in the room just became a blur, she was my focus.

It is amazing how the energy of everything works, we had this connection since the Friday so the wheels were in motion for me to pass on the message to her from her beloved grandmother. It was a major confidence boost for me as well as a kick up the ass to trust myself. I was feeling, I was seeing, I was listening and I was trusting what I was doing.

Engine Failure

I was driving home one evening and the engine on my car lost all power. I struggled for four miles rolling along the road to make it to the village to the mechanic rather than pulling over and ringing the garage. If only I had taken the chance and stopped the car then started it up again it would have worked away without a convoy of vehicles behind me.

A few days later, in the exact same spot the same thing happened me. I was more clued in this time as I realised that it was spirit trying to get my attention. There was nothing at all wrong with the car but these lost souls needed help. In the exact stop where the power in my car went, there is a candle in the wall in remembrance of two people who died there, but I never took notice of that before even though I drive this road every day.

Contrary to what people believe, you will never be put in danger when you they are seeking help. Even though I have warned them not to interfere with my car, it is not like I would be driving down the motorway doing 120mph and the engine will suddenly stop. If spirit wants your attention, they will find a way to get it but you will not be put in danger.

Traffic Light Syndrome

I tend to like to reward myself after a workout, so a Mocha is always my port of call. A few days in a row when I was leaving, the lights would not turn green for me to turn right so I would end up going into the left hand lane and taking a different route home.

On the third day I was thinking there is no way this is a coincidence, three days in a row, so I pulled over the car, and rang a friend and asked if he could tap into what I was supposed to do. He told me to get back into my body and bring back my own energy. In other words, do this yourself. So, I called back my own energy and went into a meditation sitting in my car at the side of the road. Right before my eyes I could see the big blue house that I can see from the traffic lights. I was transported back in time, when there were no roads around the area. There were a lot of spirits roaming the place. None of them saw me, it was like I was invisible in their eyes, but I felt the loss that each of them suffered. They were roaming here for years, longing for their loved ones, living as if they were still alive, suffering in silence.

So, what I do in a situation like this is I open a portal, then I call on the angels and loved ones of the spirits to come and help them to transition. A warm golden light appeared, the most beautiful angel and a lady was also came with the light, to either side of them the spirits of the loved ones appeared, there were warm embracing and they moved on. Before I came out of it, I asked to leave the portal open for another few hours in order for others in the area to see it and move on.

Another stand out incident in the area, was when I was called to help a family from years ago, 18th century I would be reckoning. If I remember correctly, the husband committed suicide after his wife and child had died during childbirth. I remember seeing the heartbreak on the father's face, you could see and feel how lost and inconsolable he was since the passing of his wife. He really truly loved her with all his heart and didn't know how he could continue on without her.

They had another child who was older, and this was the child who I was called to help. After he died his spirit stayed in the place years after his parents moved on. He never got over the tragic loss of his family.

From my understanding parts of your energy (parts of your spirit) can stay behind when you die, it doesn't mean that all your spirit is here, just certain areas of your life that you never dealt with when you were living, but you are now looking to connect it all back together again.

Swimming Smells

When I was in the middle of, what I call "coming home to myself", different stuff started happening to me. One of the main things was when I would be swimming I would start smelling different odours as some people entered the pool or even the vicinity, even as they were coming into the car park. Everyone knows that it is not possible to smell when your head is under the water, and I only come up every 4 or 5 strokes. It wasn't that these people were dirty, or spraying themselves like a lynx ad before hopping in for a dip.

So, what I was actually smelling was different spirits coming through to the people as well as different illnesses that these people were suffering from. When I am swimming I go into a complete meditative state, I am at home in the water so I have to dedicate a certain length of time to swim for otherwise I would keep going for the day.

Once I discovered what it was that I was smelling, I was able to tune in and help the spirits if they needed help. When it came to the illnesses, I would have my guides chat to the persons guides, send the energy and it would get delivered in whatever way the person needed it. The help was that it could show up in them and they realise that they needed to go to see a doctor, get a checkup, go to an energy therapist, etc.

You have to be very careful when it comes to these matters, I could not just approach random strangers and say this is what I do, I detect this in you, you could frighten the life out of people and send them into a worse state of mind. So, the guides and the angels would do the work then. I was there to channel between them. I cannot infringe on people's privacy and I cannot get too involved in people's business when it has got nothing to do with me.

Another day I was sitting in the jacuzzi chatting to a family friend who was telling me about all these symptoms that she was suffering from, immediately I could see coeliac written over her head. I knew she was open to this, and she knew what I would be up to so I told her she was coeliac. She said she was tested for it and that she isn't. I just told her she would want to get tested again because she is. A few days later she rang my mother and she was in hospital where she just found out that she is coeliac.

I would also start detecting bad energies about 5 minutes before they would appear. In particular one man, I would know he was due as I could smell the bad vibes a few minutes before he would come into the swimming pool. This was to guarantee I protect myself.

Ghosts of the past

I was asked one evening about a newly refurbished restaurant and why it wasn't performing like the owners hoped it would. When you walked through the door it was the deadest looking place you could imagine. The walls were as old as time. The vastness of the small building was big, every picture on the wall was like a memorial to the dead (also they were all black and white), there was no life, there was no colour, it was cold, everything was hollow, hard and the echo was excruciating. There was nothing homely or welcoming about it.

Truth be told it was representing the owners state of mind. The one thing that was missing was a picture of the lady who built this place up. For without her the place would never have existed. This was and is the key to the change.

The story went that the now owner did not get on with the original and even though everyone else who mattered was paid homage to, she wasn't.

It kept bringing me back to the old saying of
"you have to honor the dead". There was no way she was going to allow this business be a success without her picture on the wall, rightly so as they always said it was a family business.

What I said at the time was that, for this place to be a success, a picture has to be put up or else she will rip the floors up. A few months passed, the business was never a success, and the floorboards started to raise in the middle of ground, then it was discovered that there was a gas leak underground.

Alarm Bells Ringing

The room that I was working out of prior to Covid used to be rented out to various different people. Obviously with so many different things going on, different therapists and clients using the facilities, you would have various different energies combining, and not everyone cleans up after themselves.

When Covid came and the lockdowns ensued, everything had to be cancelled. A few weeks after the first lockdown, the alarms in the building started playing up and constantly being set off. The owner kept getting them checked and there was actually nothing wrong with them. When it was said to me, I had a different opinion on what was happening so I went in to check it out.

This is how the story goes, there was a lady booked in to see a therapist before Covid happened, lockdowns ensued and everything was cancelled. The deceased brother of the lady who was booked in had come through for her session. This was his time for closure. The appointment was made, he turned up ready and waiting. The weeks went on and he started growing more frustrated as he did not know why she wasn't showing up, he was trapped and waiting for her, that is when he started setting off the alarms to get attention.

When the alarm technicians couldn't find anything wrong, that is when I realised that it was energetic. As soon as I went in, I realised what and why it was after happening. I was able clear his energy and set about giving him the closure that he needed. It also solved the problem of the alarms being set off.

TOUGH DAY AT THE OFFICE

I had a client come to me one day, and she wanted her friend to sit in on the session with her. I don't think she knew what it was exactly that it is that I do or what she really needed, on top of it there was also a complete language barrier.

It was the toughest session I ever did and had to stop after 30 minutes. I could feel the blocks that were there and this girls energy couldn't handle a full hour, she would need shorter more frequent sessions to build her energy back up and she definitely did not need her" friend" there. She didn't want to be there herself either so that block was also there. She felt like her friend was helping her, but her friend was a leach and draining her, I sensed it straight away when they arrived and kept being shown it during the session, but I had no way of telling the girl when her "friend" is sitting right there in the room next to her. Her friend was loving the drama attached to this girl and was feeding off of it, she wasn't there to help her, she was there to make herself feel good.

The girl's partner was after dying a few months previous, and she automatically thought that he would come through during the session. This is not always the case, we can never choose who comes through. You can set the intention of who you want to show up or what you want to hear, but that does not mean that will happen, who shows up and who or what you need comes through on the day, and can be completely different to who you want or what you want to hear.

I was able to give a lot of very accurate information in the short time, but I kept being knocked back for what I said, even though when I would question it, what I was saying was being validated, it was just like they were out to prove me wrong. I had to stop the session early as it was of no benefit to anyone. There were little comments being thrown about, and I was not going to allow myself be disrespected in my own place, when all I am saying and doing is correct.

If this was a few years previous, I would of been totally knocked and my confidence would of been completely shattered. For me, this was a lesson to show me how far I have come and to trust myself, it was a lesson that I am not responsible for what comes through, I'm just responsible to deliver the message. What people take from it at the end of the day is up to them, if they are given very accurate information and details, it is up to them what they do with it, not me.

Modern Day Cult

I got a message off a person, who I will call Bill, whom I had not seen in years, I wouldn't of had much to do with him before, but I would of known him. He messaged me on Instagram and I sent one message back, nothing major, all short and sweet, or so I thought.

I was like a complete antichrist for the following few days, I was even giving out about a friend who realistically you couldn't give out about. I was really mad and angry at her for no reason, what I wasn't calling her was no one's business, my energy was completely all over the place, I was as negative as anything, even though I knew this wasn't my energy, it was so dark, and even though I know my own energy pretty good, I didn't know at the same time that this wasn't my own energy. It was just pure trickery, manipulative, sneaky and dark, I never felt energy like it before but it was after creeping inside of me.

A couple of days later, I got a text off another person, who we will call Elle, asking did I know the person who texted me, and I was like a antichrist over that too as I knew she knew the person and was thinking she was up to something when asking me, thinking that she was trying to make a fool out of me.

Shortly after that message, I was cutting the grass, then the "aha" moment eventually clicked in, it was the person who messaged me, Bill, it was their energy that was out to get me. Elle texted me as it was after affecting her too and she sensed that it was after coming at me as well, so she texted me to make me aware of it.

So how did his energy affect me so much? To be honest, I can't remember what my state of mind or energy was when he messaged me, but his energy was so strong and powerful, all it needed was for me to open the message for it to come through.

In regards to my attitude towards my friend, beside Bill contacting me, my friend was after going for a session with him also, so what was coming up in me was to make myself aware of his energy and show me that I had to protect myself even more, but also I had to make her aware of it.

The things that he told her that she would have to do was just completely ridiculous, it was just complete scaremongering. He was scaring people into continuing sessions with him other wise this or that was going to happen to them if they don't, he says he will show them the light, he tells them they are possessed by certain energies that only he can clear for them. It is just completely mind boggling and dangerous stuff that he is doing.

He is preying on the vulnerable and attaching himself as a hero who can fix them.

Instead of uniting, he was dividing, people were walking away from friendships and jobs, all just because he told them to. These were not just ordinary every day people that were caught up in his teachings, these were people from various different backgrounds, who were very self aware and had spent a lot of time working on themselves for years, they were very involved in self development but now they were back to square one, thinking what they did for the past few years was pointless and that they no longer needed the people that they had helped them up until this point.

A THORN IN MY SIDE

I was after organising a jam packed weekend for a very well-known reader, and during the weekend he was complaining of a sore neck. He went for an acupuncture treatment but that didn't shift it either.

Everything was running smoothly with appointments and the excitement around the place was smashing but I could still feel the energy was a bit all over the place, something just want right. When he finished for the day, I knew I had to go in and clear the energy, something was just feeling off to me but I could not quite put my finger on it.

On the Saturday I was chatting to his partner who said they kept getting phone calls from another center who wanted to book them. Instantly I realised that it was the energy from the other center that kept coming in, that's what I could sense when I felt something was feeling off to me. When I checked I kept being told by my guides "a pain in my neck, a thorn in my side" as proof of where the energy was coming from.

Ironically a person from the other center wanted to do a weekend where I was and was jealous that this weekend was happening. Was it just a coincidence that they kept ringing that very same weekend to book them? No, that was their way of getting their energy into the place and taking over. It was like an energetic sabotage.

Before they left on the Saturday evening he said "I still have that pain in my neck" to which his partner replied "get out, you are a thorn in my side." I was like Joey out of friends when he realised that Chandler and Monica were together, there was my validation that I was right - a pain in my neck, thorn in my side.

Now I had to figure out how I could say it. The opportunity came up on the Sunday when he asked me about the other place, if I knew it and the people running it, I just said "well that's the pain in your neck, you are being strangled as they want to be here instead of you". His face was in a bit of shock, but the pain in his neck went instantly when I made him aware of it.

MEDITATIONS

Just think of energy like a thumbprint, anything that you touch you will leave your print on, so with energy every conversation that you have, every person that you meet, every place that you go, you are constantly exchanging energy and leaving bits of your energy with them whilst taking parts of their energy with you.

The Callback

(10-15 minutes)

Close your eyes and take notice of any thoughts, feelings and sensations that are coming into your mind, body and spirit. Do not worry about them, just let them come, relax and let go.

Now start to take notice of how you feel and pay attention to the particular area that you are feeling it.

Move on to concentrating on your breath, as you inhale call back all pieces of your own energy and as you exhale release anything that is not yours.

Take notice of how the energy feels in your body as you call it back, feel the power returning to you and as you release the energy that is not yours, take notice of the sensations that arise and how you start to feel.

Now take the first colour that comes into your mind, and as you breathe in, let that colour fill up every part of your body, bringing it strength and peace.

When you feel you are ready tap your chest 3 times and open your eyes.

HOME IS WHERE THE HEART IS (45-60MINS)

Breathe and sit into your own energy, see how you feel, check out any aches, pains and emotion's that you may be experiencing and for the time being just acknowledge them.

As you are breathing start calling back your own energy as you inhale and when you exhale release anything that is not yours.

Start to imagine a light coming over you down through the crown of your head, lighting up your whole body and everything around you.

You are now going to find yourself in a room in your own house, have a look around , everything is the same, exactly the way you left it, there is no one in the house but you.

Walk out the door, into the garden and it looks exactly the same except that there is a forest down the back, the sun is not shining, it is foggy and overcast, you can feel the mist upon your skin.

You are going to walk down the path, take notice of anything you can hear or see.

Take your time then you are going to come to a bridge and walk over it and you see a door in the middle of the trees, just look at the door and see if there are any symbols or words on it.

When you are ready, the door is going to open and you are going to step in. As you look around you realise that this is exactly the same place as the other side of the door but the sun is shining, there is no fog and the birds are singing loudly.

You can see a light coming towards you and you feel safe, this is your spirit guide for this journey. As they get closer to your pay attention to any sensations or feelings that you may be having. This is their energy and your energy combining. Now they are going to lead you over the bridge and back up a path.

When you reach the end of the path you are going to come to a house, it is your house but it's buzzing with white energy flying off it, you are going to walk in, remember there is no need to knock as this is yours, as you enter take notice of how you feel, how the house feels
and have a look around.

You are now going to go into your favourite room and relax for a few moments, then your guide is going to bring you a drink. As you drink it, feel it nourishing all your body as it enters your blood stream.

Lie down and we are going to invite in a team of angels, spirit guides, ancestors and let them do the work. Take notice of anything that springs to your mind, thoughts, colours, words, pictures, and do not worry about them. All you have to do is breathe and relax.

When you are finished, your guide is going to come, place a hand on your heart and another on your head. Take notice of how this energy is feeling in your body and when you are ready, they are going to help you sit up.

As you sit up you notice something left on your lap, it a present so have a look at it and hold it up to your heart. Take notice as you look at the present of any words, images or thoughts that come to your mind. This is exclusively for you.

You can hear noise coming from another room in the house, so you are going to go check it out. See how you feel, who pops into your mind, have a look around.

Your guide is going to appear at the door now and is calling you as it's time to leave, as you ready to walk out the door you see an envelope with your name on it, open it up and read it then read it again, check the bottom of it to see if it is signed. Take notice of anything that comes into your head as you are reading.

Your guide is now going to walk you back down the path, all the ways over the bridge and to the door. When you get to the door your guide is going to place a hand on your shoulder before they slowly disappear.

As you walk through the door and back up the path, you realise that it is a completely different day to earlier, the fog and mist are gone, the sun is shining, the birds are singing and the place is full of colour. When you reach your house you are going to walk in and sit in your favourite spot, you close your eyes and feel a light come over you and bring you back into you.

Past, Present and Future

You are going to find yourself in a room where there are 3 doors.

One is going to represent the past which is everything prior to now.
The second will represent the present which is right now, what is going on in your life.
The third door will represent the future, everything that lies ahead.

Become the person or watch from above, there might be a guide there with you, but just enjoy it, see what comes up for you and do not worry about it.

Take your time and breathe, when you are ready you are going to go up to the first one that has the past written on it. When you walk inside you are going to walk down the stairs. Just take notice of how you feel as you walk through the door, is this person still you and if there are parts of this person clinging on to you.

You are going to walk down a stairs and notice what you are shown, who turns up, what the situation is. Just spend some time here and let yourself be shown what you have to be shown.

When you are leaving the room, you are going to lock the door and throw away the key, it no longer has to be visited, and do not worry about what came up for you,
it is coming up to be healed.

Now you are going to walk up to the second door which is clearly marked the Present. When you go inside you are going to walk along a corridor until you come to a room. This is all about how you are now, how you feel this present moment, what is going on in your life at present, so let the energy show you what you need to know or do. When you come out you are going to just close the door but not lock it. You are going to put the key in your pocket.

The third door is clearly marked the future.
Go in with open arms and an open mind. Take notice of how you feel, what you are shown and most importantly you are going to walk up a stairs, with optimism. Ask questions and set the intention of what you want to see, this future is represented by your current path and actions. When you are ready to leave you are going to walk out the door and if it is what you want, you are going to leave the door open but if it is not what you want, I want you to close the door.

Take a few moments in this area to gather your thoughts then when you are ready I want you to walk back to the first door with past written on it. When you walk down the stair I want you to take notice of how you feel and when you get to the bottom of the stairs you are going to be shown a situation or a person who is draining your energy. Just simply observe how this situation has a hold on you and watch why it is limiting you right now in the present.

When you are ready you are going to look around the room and find a plug with a socket plugged into it, and when you feel the time is right I want you to unplug it from the socket, this is what is holding you back or has a hold on you, so when you unplug it I want you to feel all your energy coming to you.

Just stand there and feel the room brightening up. When you are ready you are going to walk back up the stairs and when you leave you are going to close that door and lock it as the past is now completely in the past. And I want you to place the key somewhere in the room.

You are now going to walk outside into the most beautiful garden and walk barefoot on the grass until you feel the urge to lie down somewhere.

Just let yourself relax here for a few moments.

When you feel ready you are going to walk back inside and see
what has replaced the key where you left it and
hold whatever it is up to your heart,
and feel it in your heart as you breathe.

Relax and Let Go

We are going to guide you to a place of pure relaxation and then we are going to hitch it up a bit, your guide is going to come through, do not worry if you do not see them, but they are here for you, when you call them in take notice of any difference in your body, sensations, emotions, hot or cold, what colours are around you.

Then they are going to bring forward someone or show you a situation that has hurt you - even just something small but your body is still holding on to it, and it is affecting you to this day. When you are presented with this person or situation take notice of what part of your body there are any sensations or an uneasiness in, go back to see the whole story.

Then you are going to take a look in the mirror to see what blocks you yourself have put up which are affecting you, it could be something that you did, or said or feel guilty about.

Remember everything that has happened should not affect you today, you are a totally different person, and we are changing every minute. See why it still has a hold on you and ask to know how you can let it go.

Breathe and sit into your own energy, take notice of how you feel, any aches or pains, emotions and just acknowledge them.

As you inhale call back your own energy and as you exhale release anything that is not yours

Take the colour of the chair or the mat that you are sitting or lying down on, and as you breathe in you are going to breathe in this colour, letting it fill up your whole body. You were drawn to this colour, this space for a reason.

Then you are going to come back and have a look at a situation unfold, this is something that even if you do not realise it, still hurts you until this very day. Come back relax for a few moments.

Now just relax, all you have to do is breath and enjoy the energy, let it take over. Watch all the different colours coming in over you. Feel the gentle energy entering your head, just enjoy it, then feel it traveling down to your throat, then your heart, then your belly, down your legs, and then in to your feet. Now feel like there are hands on your head, your heart and your feet, keeping this energy flowing throughout your body.

When they are finished your spirit guide is going to come to your side and place a hand on your head and another on your heart.

Feel their energy combining with yours.

Feel how safe, relaxed and at peace you are.

You are now going to find yourself back in the place where you started with your spirit guide, just relax here for a few moments before you finish up and see how you are feeling, what you are seeing, hearing.

Notice the change in You since you first started.

Whirlwind Power

Picture yourself standing in the middle of a field with your eyes closed and you are simply just breathing, you can feel the breeze all around you.

You notice the breeze is getting stronger and stronger while you are still standing here with your eyes closed.

Now there is a hurricane sweeping up all around you and you end up standing in the middle of it, you are the eye and nothing is moving you.

You open your eyes to look around and everything is swirling around you.

All your troubles, doubts, fears, insecurities are now in the hurricane but yet you are calm in the middle of it.

Just enjoy this feeling for a few moments and let anything or anyone that is troubling you be swept up into the hurricane. Feel the release as it is all being swept away and swirling around you.

Now be conscious of your inhale breathe and as you exhale you raise your hand, lick your fingers and the hurricane disappears.

You are still standing in the middle of the field but now the sun is shining down on top of you, pure blue skies, no breeze and you can hear the birds singing, see how at peace you are.

Know that you have the power inside of you to choose how you react to anyone or any obstacle that gets on your way.

Superhero Strength

Close your eyes and picture yourself standing on the top of a mountain, with your hands on your hips, you feel strong, confident and proud glancing out on the world right in front of you.

Breathe in through your nose and out through your mouth, have fun with it, picture yourself as Superman, Wonder Woman, or as the strongest person that you know.

Just feel the energy entering you as you breath in, feel the power inside yourself growing stronger with every breath you take. With every breath you take you feel your power coming back to you, you can feel your body getting stronger, your mind is more focused and calm.

Breathing with Colour for Strength and Clearing

Close your eyes and relax.

As you inhale call back all parts of your energy.

As you exhale release anything that is not yours.

Now pick the first colour that comes to your mind.

As you breath in, feel this colour entering your lungs with your breath.

Now let the colour travel all throughout your body.

Starting with your head, moving it onto your neck / throat area

Then your Chest

Your heart

Your stomach

Down each leg

Your knees

Your feet

Now concentrate on your heart and let the colour travel all throughout your body, feel the colour coming down through your head and up through the soles of your feet, traveling all throughout your body.

When your whole body is full let it light up all outside your body. Relax in this feeling for as long as you like.

Problems with other People

(2 techniques)

1. Picture yourself and that person in a room together then put a big mirror up in front of you and walk away. Take yourself out of the situation, so that anything that is being directed at you is being straight away reflected right back at them.

2. Take a few moments to breathe and sit into your body. As you are inhaling start becoming aware of your breath and how you are feeling. As you inhale call back all parts of your energy that is not with you and as you exhale release any energy that is not yours.

It might also be helpful to use two different colours and make it more visual, one for your energy and one for everything that is not yours. So when you are inhaling picture the colour white filling you up and when you are exhaling picture the colour yellow leaving your body.

Journey to Meet Spirit Guides, Angels and a Healing session

Breathe and sit into your own energy, see how you feel, any aches or pains, emotions and for the time being just acknowledge them.

Breathe in your own energy and when you breathe out release anything that is not yours

Imagine a light coming over you, down through the crown of your head, lighting up your whole body and everything around you.

The light is then going to transport you to a middle of a forest. Walk around the forest, look at what you can see, listen to what you can hear, and check what you can smell.

Now follow the direction of the wind or the birds and it will bring you to a lake.

Just listen to the water slowly moving, look around and listen to the birds singing in the trees.

Now you begin to notice a light in the distance, walk towards it, this is your spirit guide for this journey. They are going to hold your hand as you fly through the sky.

Look down at the world below you, feel how free and amazing you are. Start having a bit of fun and start turning it from night to day and watch everything as you move along.

You are now going to come to a vortex, full of different colours, and your spirit guide is going to take you through it. At the other end of the vortex is an amazing house and gardens. You are going to slowly walk up to the house and take a moment and look at what is written on the door. The door will open when it is time for you to go inside.

As you enter the house, you are going to be lead to the first room which is full of books, you are going to take a book with your name written on it, and read that page, take your time.

When you are finished reading the book you are going to go on to the next room which is like a pharmacy full of natural herbs and potions, you are going to take one with your name on it.

You are going to move on to the next room, and lie down on the couch. There are an army of angels going to come in around you, offering you healing energy, feel it swirling throughout your body, from your head to your toes, giving you strength, peace and joy all at once.

When they are finished, you are going to notice that they left a gift for you on the table in the corner of the room, when you are ready, go over and see what it is, hold it up to your heart. It could be a word, a crystal, just something that you need at this time.

When you are ready you are going to get up and walk outside to the garden. Take notice of who is walking with you, what you see and what you hear. Ask questions about anything you want to know and listen for the answers.

When you are ready your spirit guide is going to come, and take you into the kitchen, take notice of what is cooking, any smells you get that are familiar, have a poke around, be nosey and look into the cupboards, take notice if there is anything that is familiar to you as this is a way of showing you who is with you.

Then have a look around the rest of the house, take notice of the pictures on the walls, ornaments.

Now your spirit guide is going to walk you back out the way you came in and fly through the tunnel of colour with you.

Now night turns to day and day turns to night until you find yourself back at the lake where you are just going to sit and relax for a few moments. When you are ready you are going to get up and walk back into the forest where you will find the light that brought you here, then you are going to let that light fill your body again with every breath you take and bring you back into this room.

BODY TALK

Go to a part in your body and listen to what it has to say to you. Take your time in each area, take notice of what area you are more relaxed in, more frustrated in, where the energy is high or low. Ask questions and your body will answer.

In each area see how you feel, so all you really have to do is breathe, do not panic with anything that comes into your head, it is just making you aware of how you are, your emotions, your thoughts and your feelings, so check out the energy. You might get some brilliant information about what your body needs, what you need spiritually, or if there are any ties to be cut.

Then when you reach the feet, be aware of any sensations going on back up your body, you are going to use colour then and you are going to feed that it to each area as you come up.

See how you feel, what is the energy like,
ask questions, if there is block,
is there anything that you need to take, etc.

Head - what is going on in it, trust what you hear, any tension, headaches, sensations, etc. just them it go.

Neck - any pains?

Throat - check if there are any blocks, if there is anything that needs to be said, ask why you have not said it.

Shoulders - is there a weight on them? Do they feel loose? Are you carrying the weight of the world? Other people's problems? Who is supporting or not supporting you?

Chest - Any restrictions? How is your breathing? Ask yourself why and what can you do about it.

Heart - how is it beating, how does it feel, see who comes into your mind, is there any ache here.

Belly - how are you feeling? Any nerves or excitement? Why are you nervous?

Hips - they do not lie?

Knees - you can't step forward without moving your feet, check here what is holding you back.

Feet - how is your energy?

Is your energy grounded?

What can you do to better look after your energy?

From the feet up, fill your body with colour, first red, watch it coming and going in waves, then let it sit, next orange, yellow, green, blue, turquoise purple, finally cover your whole body in white.

To finish breathe in the first colour that comes to your mind then tap your chest three times..

Listen to your heart

As you are breathing, pick a colour, let it fill up your whole body, reaching every limb and lighting up the whole room around you.

Just keep breathing and relax into deeper breathing,
do not worry about what way you feel as your body starts to completely relax.

Listen to what you can hear, identify it and leave it fade into your consciousness.
Try not to hold onto any awareness of the sound.
Just let it fade away.

Bring your awareness closer to you, just around your body itself.

Become aware of the space your physical body occupies and time your breathing into that.
Listen closely to your body and hear your heart beating. Really become aware of it, this is your life source.

Ask questions and let your heart answer.

Breathing exercises

Close your eyes and just breathe.

Take notice of how you feel, what thoughts are coming into your head and just let them go.

Do not worry about them and keep breathing as you are.

After a few moments, when you are breathing, on the inhale breath call back parts of your energy that you have left behind and as you are breathing out release any energy that is not yours.

Start taking notice of how you feel as you inhale and the difference after exhaling. After a while it will just become natural and you will not have to think about what you are doing.

Continue breathing like this until you feel that you are fully you and that you have released any energy belonging to anyone else.

Fast Fire Round

HOW THE ENERGY AFFECTS THE BODY FAST

Love

Close your eyes and as you breathe, think of someone you love. See where that energy sits in your body and how it makes you feel.

Hate

Close your eyes and as you breathe, think of someone or something that you hate or despise . See where that energy sits in your body and how it makes you feel.

Excitement

Close your eyes and as you breathe, think of something that excites you. See where that energy sits in your body and how it makes you feel.

Anger

Close your eyes and as you breathe, think of something or someone that makes you angry. See where that energy sits in your body and how it makes you feel.

To shift the energy back, close your eyes and think of the person you love again, see how fast it changes the whole energy in your body.

Shake, Rattle and Throw

(2-3 minutes for kids, 5 to 10 minutes for adults)

Just place your hands on your head, close your eyes, and concentrate on your breathing for a few moments, think of anything that is troubling or worrying you
and take notice how it makes you feel.

Let it all gather up in your head and feel the energy in your head pulsing out into your hands.

After a few moments, remove your hands and shake them over your head, palms facing down.
(Removing the excess negative energy).

Then when you are ready make a fist and imagine you are throwing a ball away.

Keep your eyes closed, take a few breaths and see how you feel.

****Tips****

Do it outside. If inside make sure you are throwing the "imaginary" ball out the window.

When throwing the ball (energy) away make sure no-one else is standing in your line of fire.

For kids have a bit of fun with it, get them to imagine all their thoughts, troubles and worries as a colour that they do not like.

Emotional Balance

Close your eyes and as you breathe,
just take notice of how you feel.

See which part of your body this feeling (energy) is sitting in.

Sit with the emotion and feeling for a few moments,
see how it can affect you.

Now picture someone you love or something that makes you
happy then take notice how fast the energy clears.

Sit with this feeling for a few moments
and when you are ready open your eyes.

The Thymus Tap

The thymus gland lies just beneath the upper part of the breastbone in the middle of the chest. It is the master gland of your immune system, defending against disease and infection. Negative thinking weakens the thymus gland, whilst feelings of love, trust, gratitude and courage raises its energy.

Releases Fear

Calms the Mind and Body

Increases Life Force Energy

Increase Strength

Increase Vitality

Strengthens the Immune System

Tip - tap three times before and after a longer meditation as it opens your energy and locks in the energy that you build up.

Fast Tap 1

Close your eyes and concentrate on your breathing.

Tap this area 60 times in 60 seconds.

Fast Tap 2

Tap the area 7 counts x 7 times.

To boost your energy for the day, do it first thing in the morning when you get out of bed.

So, thank you for finding me

If it was not for all the pain, love, heartache and friendships that I have had, I would not be after finding myself.

Every time I lost someone I learned more about myself.

Every time I was betrayed I learned more about other people and more importantly I learned more about myself.

Every time my heart was broken I discovered what it meant to be in love.

Every time something was taken from me, I realised how much I wanted it or how much it was not for me.

I learned different ways to cope with every different obstacle that I was faced with. Sometimes people that were in my life were merely there for us both to learn a lesson from each-other and it is not my fault or theirs that we grew apart or went our separate ways.

I have learned that "life is as easy or as complicated as you want it to be, so it is up to you what type of life you want".

Printed in Great Britain
by Amazon